SHIFTING THE MOON FROM ITS ORBIT

ALSO BY

ANDREA MARCOLONGO

The Ingenious Language
The Art of Resilience
The Art of Running

Andrea Marcolongo

SHIFTING THE MOON

A Night at the Acropolis Museum

*Translated from the Italian
by Will Schutt*

Europa
editions

Europa Editions
8 Blackstock Mews
London N4 2BT
www.europaeditions.co.uk

Copyright © Editions Stock, 2023
First publication 2024 by Europa Editions

Translation by Will Schutt
Original title: *Spostare la luna dall'orbita. Una notte al Museo del'Acropoli*
Translation copyright © 2024 by Europa Editions

All rights reserved, including the right of reproduction
in whole or in part in any form.

A catalogue record for this title is available from the British Library
ISBN 978-1-78770-518-0

Marcolongo, Andrea
Shifting the Moon from Its Orbit

Cover design and illustration by Ginevra Rapisardi

Prepress by Grafica Punto Print – Rome

Printed and bound in Great Britain by Clays Ltd, Elcograf S.p.A

For the debt I owe to Greece

> Survey this vacant, violated fane;
> Recount the relics torn that yet remain . . .
>
> First on the head of him who did this deed
> My curse shall light,—on him and all his seed . . .
> —LORD BYRON, "The Curse of Minerva"

SHIFTING THE MOON FROM ITS ORBIT

On the last week of May, in an outdoor gear shop in Paris, I bought a camping bed, a sleeping bag, and a flashlight.

The next day I loaded my luggage, rather heavier than I'd planned, into the belly of a plane departing well before dawn. A few hours later, I was pitching tent on the cold floor of the Acropolis Museum in Athens, where I would spend the night all by myself under a waning moon.

"I've never heard of such a thing!" the guards kept telling me as I struggled to assemble the aluminum frame of my cot. No one, not a soul, had ever spent the night in the Acropolis Museum before.

They don't know, I thought, these astonished Greeks. They don't know that I can hardly believe it myself.

Really, I'm stunned. I find it surreal and almost frightening not so much that, after almost a year of being worn down by my editor, the director of the most important museum in Athens, the cultural epicenter of our civilization, as they say, had authorized such an exceptional literary adventure.

No, what shocks me is the fact that of all the people in the last 2,500 years who have fallen under the spell of this eternal country, I'm the one being given such an opportunity.

For as long as I can remember, I'd never *not* spent a night in a proper bed.

I'd never pitched a wobbly tent or lain like a mummy in a sleeping bag that smells of plastic and sweat.

My untested, coddled body had never been in contact with the bare earth and unlike that of a slimy snake could not register the vibration of other people's footsteps.

Shortly before sunset, with the care of a control freak, I arranged the few personal items that I'd brought with me on top of the air conditioner, which became my bedside table for the night: banana, water bottle, notebook, toothbrush.

Life can be baffling sometimes. Who would have guessed that my first camping experience would have been at the Acropolis Museum in Athens?

"Must be an actress," remarks one guard, who just can't figure out why I'm here tonight.

What amazes me is not his automatic association of celebrity with honor, of visibility as a form of currency that opens all doors, including those of the Acropolis Museum one night at the end of spring.

No, I'm amazed by my own realization that the guard is basically right; if I'm here, it's because I put on a good show.

Héroïne grecque read the headline in *Le Monde* upon the French publication of my book about the ancient Greek language, my first. Tonight, observing my inability to formulate a single complete sentence in modern Greek, the guards at the Acropolis Museum didn't, strangely, get suspicious, and promptly switched to English.

Some heroine, I think, babbling some pleasantry or other in today's lingua franca. To be called to defend a world from barbarism and not even know its language!

I've been ashamed of my inability to speak Greek since the very first day I became a supposed philhellene—of that and a thousand other gaps in my knowledge, a thousand other things I've failed to finish.

Tonight, the line between heroine and liar seems thin in the extreme.

The instructions were curt, the proscriptions few. Aside from vandalizing the marbles sculpted by Phidias or stealing them for profit, I can do anything tonight, or almost.

The assistant director of the museum, the director of Paris's Centre Culturel Hellénique who greeted me at the entrance, the smiling guards—they were all very friendly and kind. No one dared chastise me or even question my good intentions or irreproachable conduct.

With the service you expect from a five-star restaurant, I was shown the bathroom by the exit, which I am free to use as I please. In Mediterranean fashion, the museum directors wanted to know if I'd had dinner and offered to bring me food in case I had an attack of hunger during the night.

I had been afraid I'd be strip-searched, like I was crossing a checkpoint outside Europe, but no one has bothered to even look inside my bag or check to see if my heavy blue canvas duffle really contains a camping bed and not a hatchet or Kalashnikov.

I'm not even sure there's an alarm. I guess there is. But that doesn't matter; I don't plan on touching anything, I'm actually taking great pains to keep a safe distance between me and the marbles lest I cause an accident. Lest I trip and fall and drag these eternal stones with me into the circle of mortals condemned, like me, to oblivion.

But it could be them, the marbles looking on, who'll expose me as an impostor.

And take revenge.

When the last night guard finally goes off to make the rounds of the floor below, leaving me alone with the friezes and metopes commissioned by Pericles, my hands itch to take out the only book that I've brought with me tonight. If anyone discovered what it was, I'd die of shame.

I haven't brought Homer or Plato with me, as one might expect of a so-called upstanding philhellene.

The only book I felt compelled to read in bed beside what little remains of the Parthenon marbles in Athens is a biography of Lord Elgin.

What strange machines human beings are. Give them bread, water, a little wine on occasion, and with that fuel they produce tears, laughter, dreams. And oftentimes lies.

In the lost and wholly imagined paradise that classical Greece has become for Western Europeans, there's nothing older than the Acropolis. Yet I myself predate this museum where I'm preparing to spend the night, stretched out on a camp bed.

I've entered just as the museum is getting ready to celebrate its thirteenth birthday. It's a child, barely a teen, though it took over forty years to build; the first public competition dates to 1976. The giant, modern building, based on a design by the Swiss architect Bernard Tschumi and the Greek architect Michalis Photiadis, wasn't inaugurated until 2009, after years and years of work and projects scratched, because in Athens the past emerges from underneath the earth, like lava in the form of archaeological remains.

This must partly explain why I always seem to notice a veil of melancholy over the eyes of Greeks: they are a people forbidden to forget.

Like Sisyphus, they've been forced to remember for millennia.

Except the stone they have to roll isn't headed to the top of the mountain, but forever emerges from below it.

15 Dionysiou Areopagitou, for Dionysius the Areopagite, the patron saint of Athens. That's the museum's address, should I be so lucky as to receive mail tonight. Should I want to send something, I've already noted a mailbox right next to the entrance, which cheered me up about the state of the world, like those mailboxes by the sliding doors at airports, forgotten monoliths of red iron erected long ago, that you can find next to modern machines for wrapping suitcases in cellophane.

I'm thinking of people who visit the Acropolis Museum and buy a postcard of the Caryatids or the Moschophoros in the gift shop on the ground floor and are suddenly so eager to mail it that they can't bear to wait for the time it would take to find a post office. As if all of life were worth a single, licked stamp.

I know that overwhelming sense of urgency. Outside this museum there's someone I've been writing a postcard to once a week for years.

Before getting here tonight, I bought one.

Because it isn't so much a matter of protecting the past but saving the present moment from the future.

My appointment with the assistant director of the museum was scheduled for eight o'clock, just before sunset. I came on foot, my hotel being close by in the white-and-blue, touristy kaleidoscope of Plaka. Its name, the Hotel Byron, seemed to me a sign, a portent of the story I want to tell, almost as much as the omission of *lord* before the name of the English poet and forebear of philhellenism pointed to the modesty of my accommodations.

A smiling Anna was waiting for me at the entrance, at the top of stairs that sink, cavea-style, down to the archaeological site below the museum—hence the enormous pillars holding it up. I read somewhere that the pillars are lodged deep in the bedrock of Athens, like reinforced concrete tusks, and can protect the ruins of the Acropolis from a magnitude ten earthquake.

These precautions against geological disaster are no doubt necessary, but I'm not so sure the land that produced the classical world represents its greatest threat; I fear it's the carelessness of the men and women who have inherited the classical world that will soon generate the ultimate earthquake that will reduce the remains of ancient Greece to rubble.

We'll have destroyed so much we ourselves will become the ruins.

Introductions were curt, as if we were in a hurry to go out to meet a night unlike any other, and therefore destined to pass quickly.

They didn't even ask me for ID. Not a document or a photo that certifies that this pale face that I carry with me is really mine.

It wouldn't have mattered had another woman shown up in my place and claimed she was me.

But after all, the star of tonight's show is the Acropolis, same as it is every night. Like all the puny and awestruck mortals who have marched around her feet gazing up, I'm just a walk-on, destined to disappear.

They trust me, the Greeks. They trusted me from the start, beginning with my first book. They never asked any questions.

They should have.

We all know what happened the last time a foreigner showed up at the Parthenon with a big smile and the best of intentions.

He carted it off, carted it off to London.

To resell it.

25,000 square meters. That's how much space I'll have for the next twelve hours. Not bad compared to the barely twenty square meters with a view of Montmartre that I've owned for a few years. One night, a few years ago, as we were celebrating my signing the deed, a friend said cheerfully, "You bought a house in Paris by writing books about Greece—genius!" I didn't laugh.

Ever since that night I've had the sticky feeling, like a cold sweat, that the purchase of my first home, maybe the only one I'll ever own, is the result of my having somehow exploited Greece.

Or robbed it "with dexterity"—as the Italian legal term calls it when a thief commits a crime with particular skill, cunning, or imagination.

For years everyone's congratulated me: "How did you get it into your head to write a book on Greek? What an original idea."

It's true, I was resourceful. Like a thief.

Novelty in whatever form is met with intolerance in Athens.

Anyone over twenty visiting the *new* Acropolis Museum can't help but compare it to the *old* one. The one that used to be on the Acropolis, a lovely little brick house on the east side of the Parthenon.

Built in 1863, just thirty years after the last Turkish garrison departed, the old museum quickly became too small to house the works being unearthed during the excavation campaigns.

I remember reverently visiting it the first time I climbed up to the Acropolis, a seventeen-year-old on a school trip.

I also remember its being so ordinary that I mistook it for the restroom.

I was given no guidance as to where exactly to set up my cot tonight.

I didn't ask, nor did the assistant.

To everyone, myself included, my spending the night on the third floor beside the marbles of the Parthenon must have seemed so completely normal that it wasn't even worth questioning.

I know the museum, have visited it on various occasions, and each time I've found it more beautiful and heartbreaking.

Each time emptier.

Tonight I didn't even bother to look around the ground floor, where the remains of the other buildings that once sat on top of the Acropolis are, or the first floor, where the works of art are exhibited. The Caryatids discovered around the Parthenon, which once adorned houses and temples, are the standout. I immediately rode the escalator up to the Phidian marbles, as if that were the natural place to start.

As if it were my home.

I hadn't thought about it for years. I'm loath to think of the gloomy, tortured girl I was, yet tonight, as I ascend to the top floor of the Acropolis Museum, I recall something one of my Greek university professors used to say. On the rare, dreaded occasion I bumped into him in the elevator, he'd always ask me, tickled by a joke that I fear fewer than a handful of people would get nowadays, "*Anabasis* or *katabasis*?"

Up or down?

The Greek hero of anabasis (also the title of his best-known work) was Xenophon, who described the difficult march up country to Greece's blue sea by ten thousand Greek soldiers in the pay of Cyrus who had been lost in the desolate lands of Persia. Whereas the first—as is always the case with the Greeks, the first *ever*—to dare make a katabasis to the realm of the dead was Odysseus, who, during his long wanderings, having reached the country of the Cimmerians at the edge of the Ocean, descends to Hades to meet the prophet Tiresias and, more importantly, his mother, Anticlea, who died of grief.

The slow escalator makes me a crude deus ex machina, come tonight to disturb the tragic stillness of Phidian's sculptures.

Going up, I see the Caryatids flowing under my feet, shielded by the clear glass floor, like locusts trapped in formaldehyde.

Will my night be an anabasis or a katabasis?

I can't help wondering whether I'm traveling back home, to Greece, the country I have publicly sworn my allegiance to, only to betray it for a handful of crumbs and a new book contract. Just like Cyrus' mercenaries. Or whether I am descending into a hell all my own, one that I myself perversely invented.

The same descent into hell that Lord Elgin, blinded by Greekness and full of good aesthetic intentions, made two hundred years ago and would spell his ruin.

Besides forever reducing the Parthenon to rubble, naturally.

"It wasn't my destiny that brought me here," says Zorba the Greek, "but I who brought my destiny."

I don't know when my destiny began, but tonight, at the Acropolis Museum in Athens, I have the impression that I simply let myself be dragged along by it.

From the very beginning, from the first word that I shyly scribbled in Greek as a little girl.

I'm not Greek. Nor am I French, though I've been obsessed with belonging to France for the last few years.

Even if I pretend otherwise, restraining my gestures and muffling the accent that I've inherited from my native land, I am, first and foremost, Italian.

It wasn't a professional opportunity that brought me to Paris, nor did I move for love. I can hardly claim to have been driven from my homeland by war, natural disaster, or economic crisis. If I left Italy, it's because I wanted to.

I'm almost ashamed to admit it, but choosing to be an exile represents the supreme affront, an unacceptable outrage to those who have had to flee their land because of a tragedy that couldn't be borne. My own story, on the other hand, is pure comedy.

Boredom and whimsy made me a migrant.

Opera. Venice. Pasta. Botticelli. Fashion. Dante. Those are

the responses I get in France whenever I say I'm Italian. *La dolce vita*.

Not once have I felt an ounce of pride, as if all that beauty had anything to do with me. I recognize it, I'm grateful for it, but in no way do I feel that it is a part of me just because I have Italian blood pumping in my veins.

What I feel about Italy today is not a sense of pride but rather a sense of desertion.

I'm the kind of Italian abroad who doesn't cook spaghetti or tiramisu. Who, at parties, doesn't sing Domenico Modugno or Raffaella Carrà. Sometimes I pretend not to know the words! Who doesn't ache to return to Capri or Florence or have restaurant recommendations and secret travel tips to share. Who hasn't read an Italian paper in years in order to shield herself from being embarrassed by the biggest showmen in European politics and who is almost more ashamed of the twenty-year reign of Berlusconi than of the cliché about the country being all "pizza, mafia, mandolin."

I am, in short, the kind of Italian abroad who feels that by some miracle she's avoided the enormous peril of caricature.

What prevents many immigrants from learning more of their adopted country's language than simple phrases to use in daily exchanges and absorbing what schoolbooks refer to as "local customs and traditions" is the irrational hope that they are really just passing through. The belief that the crisis that drove them to leave home and country is no more than one of the many accidents that stain a life and will soon be resolved, making the return home natural.

Like a tourist on a two-week vacation in some exotic locale who doesn't bother to learn the language and blend in with the locals, many migrants, no matter their social class, believe integration is a useless pursuit and that one day they'll go back home, even decades on.

That's not a life; it's passing the time. Like an insect that's sure she'll recover the shell she shed.

But I came to France to stay.

In fact I did everything to slip out of the shell of my country and blend in as much as possible with the French. To wash away the green in my Italian flag and repaint it *bleu*.

Maybe for me Greece is no more than what psychologists call an act of transference, I think, watching the May sun dip below the Lycabettus Hill. My relationship with Italy is so unresolved and fractured and my relationship with France still in its infancy and unconsummated that I have fashioned a third spiritual homeland, one even more exotic and distant.

Or maybe it's the age-old inferiority complex that all Italians feel toward Greece: sure, we're a country of saints, poets, and sailors, but most of all of frauds.

Rome was undoubtedly the greatest empire of the ancient world, and Caesar and Augustus the greatest strategists until the time of Churchill and De Gaulle, but our culture, which we all inherited from the Romans, is an exact copy of that of the unrivaled Greeks. *Graecia capta ferum victorem cepit*, wrote Horace. Conquered Greece conquered its savage captor. In that version of the story, the Romans are the savages. The others are cultured and refined, the contemporaries of Pericles who built the Parthenon that I find myself standing in front of tonight.

So the Romans ripped off Greece. The Italians, and all Latin peoples, including the French, have ripped off Rome. And I—French imposter, Italian defector, would-be philhellene—what am I going to falsify tonight at the Acropolis Museum?

Did I really think that by osmosis I could arrive at the crystalline truth trapped like a fossil in Phidias's marbles?

Sometimes, as if to justify my actions, I tell myself I'm Italian because I inhabit the Italian language.

I inhabit it, but I don't speak it. Since I don't have Italian friends in Paris, entire weeks can go by in France without my speaking Italian, if not in my head.

The Italian language has become my silent language, the language of my ramblings, concoctions, nagging thoughts. And regrets.

But I write strictly in Italian, even when I can or want to write in French. The Italianness of my writing is therefore a deliberate choice, one I own and pursue despite being irked by it, especially by the fact that I can't share what I write with the people around me who don't speak Italian. Other silences, other excisions, once again.

French isn't what's holding me back. Actually, I'm sure that it is only a matter of time before I start writing in French. For now I'm just stalling to put off the inevitable, final separation for as long as possible: when I stop writing in Italian, I will have severed my last ties to Italy.

It's not just a question of geography. My story isn't merely one of uprooting and disowning my country. I'm well aware that my connection to Italy would be different had I not lost both my mother and father.

My wandering lifestyle isn't the result of having no address, but of having no family to return to.

My mother died a long time ago, when I was still a child, before the museum where I'm about to spend the night ever existed. For years I have measured the depth of her absence with the technological innovations she never had a chance to know: high-speed rail, the smartphone, social networks.

My memories are distant, fuzzy, mute: I don't think I can recall my mother's voice.

My father, on the other hand, passed away recently, leaving me with the vague sense that something's missing, as if every part of my life were ringed with loss.

And betrayal. Strange as it sounds, I didn't think he'd ever die.

For me, Italy was my father. The man with whom I spoke every day, day and night, for at least thirty years. Italian was my father tongue.

The fact that every day sixty million people continue to speak it in Italy is completely irrelevant to me; without him, silence is all I need of Italian now.

Athens wasn't the first choice. As an Italian, a night at the Uffizi, the Vatican Museums, or Pompeii would have been much easier.

But I never even considered them to be options: they're all museums I know and love, but they're not me. They're not *mine*.

Cowardly, tonight I'd rather the guards of the Acropolis Museum think I'm dumb, or a liar for not speaking Greek, than have to exchange niceties all night with someone from my country.

Tonight, the prospect of speaking Italian with someone other than my father seems unbearable.

W ho knows how you'll feel with all those marble eyes staring at you the whole night," my friends told me before my departure, hoping to unnerve me.

As I wait for dusk to bring down the curtain on the lights of Athens, I realize that there won't actually be so many eyes staring at me tonight.

Quickly scanning what remains of the friezes and metopes of the Parthenon, I manage to make out a few fragments of a head, many feet, some arms, the muzzle of a horse or two. But the faces of these ageless men and women, sculpted by the school of Phidias to look at and be looked at, are no longer here. They've been swallowed up by time. Or decapitated by human greed that took those heads and made off with them.

I could have chosen from among the overstuffed and over-opulent collections in Rome, Florence, or Venice.

Instead I decided to spend the night in an empty museum.

It's not the presence of marbles I'm afraid of tonight, but their absence.

I fear that once again I have inserted myself—consciously no less—into a story about gaps, losses, lacunae.

About empty spaces and neglect.

Another of destiny's little "assaults with tear gas," as the Greek poet Giorgos Seferis wrote.

With time and faith, the hole in one's soul can be filled, or so they say. But the hole in a museum, how is that healed? Is it really just a matter of returning the work, something the Greeks have been patiently waiting for for nearly two centuries and for which they built this modern museum I find myself in tonight? Or, once excavated, does the absence become unfillable?

Is it enough to rewind the days and lies and put things back in place for everything to return to order, for the hole to finally be filled?

And by taking from one to give back to the other, are we not just creating a void somewhere else, one that wasn't there before?

A long time ago, I learned with difficulty to place my trust in signs, confident that something always comes along. And if it didn't come, that was because I didn't know how to recognize it.

More than belief, I'd call it *surrender*: sometimes I have the impression of tripping over the thin illogical threads that life weaves to reveal its meaning.

Whether by chance or fate, tonight the first marble on which my eye rests is not from Greece. Or rather: it was carved in Athens, yes, but it was brought back from Italy.

I hadn't read the news in the papers. I knew nothing about this story, one that is characteristic of the controversy surrounding the destiny of the Parthenon marbles.

So I was almost startled when, walking around the perimeter of the room to get my bearings before the long night ahead of me, I came across a glass cabinet.

When I last visited the Acropolis Museum, barely three months ago, it wasn't there.

Inside, elegantly lit and labeled with straightforward captions, is a slab of Pentelic marble (so they call the type of marble with which the Parthenon was sculpted, extracted from the mountain of the same name) that belongs to the eastern frieze and was returned to Athens from the Antonino Salinas Regional Archaeological Museum in Palermo.

The fragment is also known as the "Fagan fragment," after the English consul in Sicily Robert Fagan, who, at the beginning of the nineteenth century, had come into possession of it under circumstances that have never been cleared up. Upon his death, the marble was passed on to his wife, who promptly resold it to the museum in Palermo sometime between 1818 and 1820.

I know the Salinas. They invited me to talk about Calypso and women in Homer a few days before the world buckled under the weight of the pandemic. But I hadn't even noticed this marble then. Just two weeks before my arrival here at the Acropolis, the fragment depicting a foot, perhaps belonging to an enthroned Artemis, has come home to sit beside its mute marble brothers and sisters. They had initially envisaged it as a temporary loan, part of a cultural exchange of works between the Salinas Museum and the Acropolis Museum, but the Region of Sicily ultimately decided to make the transfer permanent and then, by a legal procedure, conceded its rights to state ownership.

Tonight, this marble returned to Athens from Italy seems like a sign. And like consolation.

I imagine the foot of Artemis, twenty-four centuries after being sculpted by Phidias, being loaded into the belly of an airplane ready to take off from the Palermo Airport, one of my favorites in the world, which faces the sea, like a baroque windowsill. I picture it traveling the same route Odysseus took to get back to Greece—only not in the water but in the sky—evading sirens, sea monsters, and irresistible nymphs.

I can almost hear the marble sigh with relief when the plane door opens and the warm air of Athens, its Ithaca in Attica, sensuously caresses it as it had for over two thousand years when it sat high atop the Parthenon.

This story of returns, of what the Greeks call *nostoi*, the word from which we get the word "nostalgia," is the first gift I've received during my night at the museum. Unexpectedly, it is the first time I feel I belong to my country, Italy.

When it comes to restitution, all eyes have been on England, but France can't ignore the matter either. In the Louvre's collection of Greek antiquities, a metope and part of the Parthenon frieze are still on display, though they often go unnoticed by visitors searching for the Nike of Samothrace or the Venus de Milo.

The metope, the tenth on the south side of the Parthenon, is simply beautiful: a wild Centaur is caught in the act of attacking a Lapith woman, her peplos overgarment flapping in the wind. The fragment of the frieze, on the other hand, represents a group of young women, known as Ergastines, participating in the procession at the Great Panathenaea festival, during which they oversaw the weaving of a precious votive peplos in honor of the goddess Athena.

The two marbles now at the Louvre were part of a collection amassed by the Comte de Choiseul-Gouffier, the French ambassador to the Ottoman court during the Napoleonic Empire, member of the Académie française, and author of *Voyage pittoresque de la Grèce*.

It was Louis-François-Sébastien Fauvel, the painter and archaeologist following the diplomatic mission, who collected a wealth of ancient works for him in Athens. Fauvel carried on a bitter lifelong rivalry with Lord Elgin and Elgin's Italian painter, Giovanni Battista Lusieri. However, unlike the English, the French never obtained the sultan's permission to climb to the top of the Acropolis, then a fortress, because the Ottomans feared that the French might spy from above on honest Turkish women.

"Take away everything you can," wrote Count Choiseul-Gouffier from Constantinople to his assistant Fauvel stationed in Athens. "Don't miss an opportunity to steal from Athens and its surroundings all that can be stolen. Spare no one, neither the living nor the dead." And Fauvel would have been more than willing to oblige had Lord Elgin and his friends not already sent the most important finds to London, including fifteen metopes, seventeen statues from the pediments, and seventy-five meters of the one hundred and sixty-meter-long frieze of the Parthenon.

An odd detail in this story of arrivals and departures, of taking and leaving, is that the fragment of the Parthenon frieze that Fauvel filched on Choiseul-Gouffier's orders remained in the basement of the Louvre until 1802—it had arrived in 1798—when Napoleon himself, bothered that France didn't possess enough works by Phidias to compete with England's unparalleled collection, demanded it be publicly displayed.

That's often how it goes: real talent isn't about finding treasure but deciding what to do with it.

Absence as the most acutely felt presence.

It is the stories of the missing marbles that interest me tonight at the Acropolis Museum, almost more than those standing silently before me, which I could reach out and touch, as if to pick an apple or a flower. I want to know where they are and, at least with words, try to fill the void left behind by the saws and picks of Europeans like me who remorselessly turned ancient Greece into their "stone shop," as Lord Byron writes in "The Curse of Minerva."

But a minute later I think, who am I to judge, unearthing from my bag my heavily underlined copy of Lord Elgin's biography. Me, who learned ancient Greek at school almost by chance, made Greece my personal idea shop, and staked my writing career—my entire life—on it.

I'm certainly not the first nor the only person to do so. All of Europe has done the same since the age of Alexander the Great.

All of us have always taken, mined, and extracted from Greece carelessly and without compunction. And for centuries we've used these plundered ideas to fashion our idea of culture and civilization.

We're pleased to claim the classics are "our roots," but in reality the tree we're so proud of is the result of what agronomists call grafting—the practice of affixing a delicate plant to the roots of a hardier one.

The fruits are the unsustainable world we inhabit today.

Like Jonah in the belly of the whale, over the last 2,500 years we've all strolled into Greece, locked the door behind us, and tossed the key into the Aegean. And ever since we've been ready to devour each other.

"You're the guardian of the Acropolis tonight," a Greek friend whom I owe a lot told me. He was being generous. He came here to take the customary photos and capture a moment which by dawn I'll have trouble believing ever happened. And yet, while I cautiously, quietly walk through the Parthenon gallery, I move with the prudent, studied gestures not of a guard but of a thief casing the joint.

Disregarding etiquette, I've taken off my shoes and deposited them beside my bed. Tonight I'm going barefoot.

Ever since Phidias put down his chisel, these marbles have lived in silence. No, they *are* the silence of an entire lost world, concentrated in these stones like succulent jade. Far be it from me to disturb them with the annoying click of my heels.

Out the colossal windows of the museum, Athens is preparing for the sleepless joy of a Saturday evening at the end of spring. Who knows if they can see me from outside, I find myself wondering, whether out of shyness or exhibitionism I can't say.

One part of me fears that this adventure of mine is just the latest example of my hubris. Another part would have everyone walking by the Acropolis tonight see me and bear witness to this privilege I've been granted. And if it was granted to me, then it means that I earned a pass. It means that Greece was naïve enough to say "Nice job" again.

I daydream of passersby carrying cold beers in their hands

or still-warm gyros and glimpsing through the windows, lit by streetlights, the silhouette of a human being wandering the halls of the Acropolis Museum. How would they react? Would they be startled? Would they think a thief was stealing the metopes of the Parthenon and promptly call the police? Or would they take it for yet another outrage, the whim of one more influencer rich enough to buy a night on the Acropolis, or a megalomaniacal attempt to seduce a mistress by someone with the right contacts, and take a blurry photo or noisy video with their phones which they would then share indignantly on some social network?

Deep down I hope so. If anyone tonight should see me, I hope they'll do whatever they fancy, no matter how crazy or sloppy, given this unprecedented situation.

I'm ready with head bowed to bear the brunt of a scandal or for the police to come barging in or to be pelted with eggs and tomatoes.

But what I really won't stand for is indifference. The prospect of no one doing anything about a foreigner once again being suspected of looting the Acropolis. Except blame the incompetent, lazy Greeks who just don't know how to protect their treasures—which, at the end of the day, are ours, more ours than theirs, so the nineteenth century archaeologists claimed, convinced they were doing Greece a favor by smuggling out their works of art to protect them in the fine museums of the West.

On the floor below, where the Caryatids shoulder an invisible weight, the guard is busy listening to the radio broadcast the Champions League final being played in Paris.

Outside, no one has thrown a fit or suspects anything.

The Acropolis serves the same function for Athens as the mirrors of Archimedes, except that, rather than focusing the sun's rays into a single point, it draws the gaze of everyone who passes by.

I'm almost disappointed to realize that no one seems to see me behind the glass, lit by streetlamps. I start waving my arms in front of the huge window overlooking Dionysiou Areopagitou while pedestrians go obliviously by. I flap my hands and hop on my feet as if I were doing gymnastics or sending up a flare. So what if they think I'm mad? I want my inappropriate presence in this museum to be revealed, as it should be.

I demand to be seen, I want to be mocked and punished if need be.

Consider it a drill, like those done by the dozens in public buildings to prepare for a fire or earthquake.

A dress rehearsal to test our ability to stay vigilant, defend the classical world, and train our reflexes in the event of imminent danger.

As always, I'm playing the part of the thief, but what worries me tonight isn't my performing the role of enemy or satyr.

No, what worries me is the possibility that those witnessing the crime might once again dismiss the looting of Greece as merely a matter of old values and old stones. "What's the big deal? If we really want to see them, we can go to London."

* * *

Not only do I have in my pocket the biography of the most famous looter of artworks ever, but bouncing around my head is Emmanuel Carrère's *The Adversary: A True Story of Monstrous Deception*. I don't even want to imagine what the director of the Acropolis Museum would think if he knew he'd handed over the keys to the Parthenon marbles to someone who delights in the stories of a thief and a murderer.

I reread *The Adversary* with a mixture of excitement and apprehension on the plane to Athens. I had my reasons for bringing it along. At one point, Carrère writes of his moral stance towards Jean-Claude Romand, a man convicted of murdering his parents, wife, and two children: "I realize that I immediately rubbed him the right way by adopting a dispassionate and compassionate gravity, seeing in him not a man who had done something horrific, but a man to whom something horrific had happened . . . "

This is exactly the stance I can't help taking toward Thomas Bruce, 7th Earl of Elgin, 11th Earl of Kincardine, who was appointed Minister Plenipotentiary and Ambassador Extraordinary of His Britannic Majesty to the Sublime Porte of Selim III, Sultan of the Ottoman Empire, in November 1798.

In the history of the Parthenon marbles, and philhellenism generally, Elgin has always been "the adversary."

From the start I've given Elgin the white-glove treatment, so to speak.

For reasons that partly escape me and are now making knots form in my stomach, it was impossible for me to completely condemn "the man who took the Parthenon marbles" (as per the subtitle of the French edition of William St. Clair's biography that I brought with me to the museum).

This is what most embarrasses me as I hold the gaze of the Acropolis: I can't blame the person whom every Greek-loving man and woman, or just anyone with a sense of honor, justifiably blames.

For two hundred years the Greeks have been demanding the rightful restitution of their marbles, but as I look at this mutilated statuary, I feel sympathy for the man who butchered them.

Elgin wasn't a murderer. He didn't kill any humans. What he did kill was the integrity of the Parthenon and the very idea of Greece, which he split apart, packed into wooden crates, and shipped elsewhere, far from the descendants of the Greeks who brought it into this world.

As the weeks and days sped by and my date with the Acropolis Museum approached, I developed a kind of morbid curiosity in the Parthenon's greatest antagonist. Almost a complacent, at times amused pity towards the man whom Lord Byron, in "Childe Harold's Pilgrimage," described as a "paltry antiquarian," guilty of having made Athens "contemptible as himself and his pursuits."

I don't know if this fascination of mine corresponds to that ambiguity between good and evil, between victim and victimizer, which often leads part of the public to sympathize with the most cold-blooded killers. Yet before I encountered Elgin's story, I never vacillated when it came to deciding who was good and who evil, who right and who wrong; I have often been proud to stand in solidarity with victims and oppressed people, and I have never felt drawn to the dark side, not even in novels.

I had always been baffled by women who, as free citizens, exchange letters with violent criminals sentenced to life in prison, and even go so far as to marry men behind bars. Then I discovered the story of Lord Elgin. And I became one of those women. In fact, at times I have the impression that I'm writing this book for him.

It isn't a love story or a declaration of my approval of his having pillaged the Parthenon, but the interrogation of an equal, one person to another.

If I write, if tonight I'm alone with the Parthenon marbles holding Elgin's biography in my hands, it is to force their despoiler to be reunited with them two hundred years after his crime and look directly at them, both at what's intact and what, especially, is missing: the severed heads, the amputated feet, the interrupted processions, the friezes so disfigured they seem to have been placed under rack and screw.

Because the story of his theft symbolizes and synthesizes the theft that all Westerners have been perpetrating against Greece for centuries.

We've always thought of the classical world as something to be extracted: a block of marble from the core of the mountain, a statue from the dry earth of Samothrace, a child from her mother's womb.

So, you're all invited to this nocturnal inquisition at the Acropolis Museum.

Let him who has never taken anything from Greece, not even an idea, cast the first stone at Lord Elgin.

> Cold is the heart, fair Greece, that looks on thee,
> Nor feels as lovers o'er the dust they loved;
> Dull is the eye that will not weep to see
> Thy walls defaced, thy mouldering shrines removed . . .
> —LORD BYRON, "Childe Harold's Pilgrimage"

Well then, my heart must be very cold, and my eye uncaring—something Byron deplored—if I struggle so hard to understand. To want to imagine.

Because if forgiving is out of the question, I want to at least try to understand.

At the start of this story are an ambitious politician in poor health, a stately home in the English countryside, and a beautiful, ambitious young wife with a cheerful disposition. In the background are Napoleon and Nelson.

In November 1798, Lord Elgin was thirty-two years old and had already distinguished himself in the three fields expected of an English nobleman: the military, politics, and diplomacy. However, the young Elgin suffered from attacks of rheumatism, which forced him to periodically take lengthy breaks from the humid continental climate and retreat to healing spas: the dry, mild climate of the Mediterranean was one of the chief reasons why he accepted a delicate diplomatic mission in the East, a region he was completely unfamiliar with.

The idea of leaving for Constantinople as Minister Plenipotentiary came not from Elgin but from the King of England himself, who worried about the fate of the campaign in Egypt that Napoleon was conducting at the time.

Bonaparte's entry into Egypt caused Turkey to declare war against France, and France's perpetual rival, England, intended to exploit the situation. This was the delicate objective given to His Majesty's new ambassador in Constantinople. To prepare for the undertaking, Elgin thought it wise to first procure a wife, to avoid his being over thirty and unmarried overshadowing his sterling diplomatic career.

A few weeks later, he decided on Mary Hamilton Nisbet of Dirleton, a young woman from a good family with great ambitions, though not of equally great substance. After the wedding the new couple (very much in love, it was said; they nicknamed one another "Eggy" and "Poll," cooingly) prepared to leave for Constantinople, which at the time was extremely exotic and worlds away, but not before commissioning an architect to renovate the small Elgin family castle at the Firth of Forth, so that it was more congenial to an honest family life than the licenses of bachelorhood.

"When you're in the East, don't forget to stop by Athens to see the ancient ruins with your own eyes." So, more or less, said Thomas Harrison, the neoclassical architect hired to remodel the residency. It had likely never occurred to Elgin to set foot in Athens.

How many unremarkable words and gestures do we produce a day? "Boy, it's hot." "Can you believe this traffic?" "Pick up some milk while you're out." Such phrases appear trivial, harmless, given, yet they have the potential to forever alter the course of a life. The importance of everything always reveals itself later; a life is understood only in hindsight.

In Elgin's case, it may have been the architect's offhand comment, tossed out while demolishing a wall or hanging wallpaper, that forever changed his destiny. He certainly didn't realize it right away. All he did was add a possible excursion to Athens to the list of the thousand other things to be done once he arrived on the other side of the Mediterranean, with the same offhandedness with which we pretend to memorize the address of a restaurant that our one, in-the-know friend insists we check out.

Who knows whether Elgin ever thought back on that moment, whether he regretted having exchanged a few cordial words with Harrison that afternoon. Whether he came to regret ever having met him. More importantly, who knows whether Elgin managed to identify that trivial suggestion as the root cause of everything. Of his personal ruin and that of the Parthenon.

Because it was that thought, by all appearances innocent, uttered in the fog of the Scottish countryside, that precipitated the curse of Minerva.

At the time—and by then for many centuries, ever since 1453, the year Constantinople fell, and with it the Byzantine Empire—Greece was under Turkish rule and was, in effect, cut off from European history.

Only recently had it become accepted wisdom that the best cache of classical architecture lay in Athens, and not in Rome, as had been believed during the Renaissance. Specialists knew the Athenian treasures through highly detailed drawings made by seventeenth-and-eighteenth-century archaeologist adventurers brave enough to go to Greece, which at the time, for geographical and in particular political reasons, was really on the other side of the world. But the true face of classical art was mostly unknown to the general European public, who could hardly imagine the majesty of the Acropolis or the perfection of the statues of Praxiteles and Polycletus.

Elgin, on the other hand, immediately began to picture it. He saw how his work in Greece could bring into being an aesthetically evolved England, one whose artistic excellence would be unsurpassed in all of Europe, with ranks of artists among the most gifted that history had ever known, toiling in the service of the Crown.

So, with enthusiasm and ingenuity, he launched himself into this noble project that would make Greece the supreme model for English art, deciding to bring a delegation of artists and archaeologists with him to Constantinople, just as Napoleon had done in Egypt.

For months the possibility of leaving for Greece on the heels of Elgin was a favorite topic of discussion at the Royal Academy of Arts, but, as almost always happens when it comes to culture, the Crown didn't allocate an adequate budget for the endeavor. Apparently even William Turner was interested in the idea, but the famous painter quickly gave it up due to a lack of funds. The British government instead assigned Ambassador Elgin a philologist, since back then lost manuscripts were the mirage of every Westerner convinced they might find an unpublished work by Plato or Aristotle languishing in some Eastern monastery.

"I'll pay for it out of my own pocket, then. What's a few shillings anyway?" Elgin must have concluded when the Crown refused to sponsor an operation of such importance, one on which the life or death of the aesthetic taste of England depended. He then decided to proceed independently, drawing on the funds of his noble family to hire at least one painter and a team of workers as soon as he arrived in Greece.

The British government's indifference toward the marbles of Athens was the second ominous sign that the ambassador failed to grasp, prelude to another disaster to which Greece would one day condemn him: economic ruin.

Preparations done and the necessary personnel hired, in September 1799 Lord Elgin set sail for Constantinople from Portsmouth Harbor, accompanied by his wife Mary, then pregnant with their first child.

As someone who sees signs everywhere, I now wonder how much Elgin knew about Greek mythology. Not much, I'm guessing, if he had no qualms with boarding a military ship named after the reckless son of Helion, Phaeton, whose childish inexperience led him to wreak so much destruction on Earth.

In the myth, Phaeton, still a child, attempts to drive Helios's chariot but immediately loses control of the horses and scorches all the unfortunate regions in his path before Jupiter strikes him with a thunderbolt. It is a story of devastation, tears, ruin. Supposedly Phaeton's sisters wept so much over their dead brother that they turned into poplar trees. To this day, in Northern Italy, the poplar's sheer white flowers, like feathers only highly flammable, are called the "tears of April."

According to the myth, Phaeton's devastating journey across the sky left behind the pyrotechnic Milky Way, which grew out of the sparks that the flames produced.

Aboard a ship that bore that name, "Eggy" was embarking on a voyage by sea that would leave in its wake white splinters of Pentelic marble and the tears of an entire nation—Greece.

I was raised by a man without an education. Not in ancient Greek nor in Latin: my father had no education whatsoever.

He didn't even speak proper Italian. Venetian dialect, from the region in which he was born, was the one language he spoke, and he swore allegiance to it for seventy-six years without ever succumbing to shame for being almost illiterate.

I was raised by a man who went to elementary school on foot, wearing hobnailed shoes with wood soles, he'd tell me, beaming at my look of astonishment.

"I was born with *sgalmare*," he told me, referring to the clogs that he wore as a child with the pride of someone who'd made it in life. If I write that dialect word in a book on the classical world and the Acropolis, it is to honor him. And to beg his forgiveness. He brought into this world a daughter who may know the ancient Greek of Homer and Plato, but who always refused to learn the crooked dialect of her father.

He was born and raised in a cluster of concrete houses flung to the ground like spare change in the countryside of Vicenza, at the foot of Mount Asiago. "The center of the world," he'd boast, as if he were born in Manhattan or Saint-Germain-des-Prés. I made fun of him for years for what I thought was nonsense, ruthless as a child who refuses to take her parents at their word.

Today, workers from Africa live in the house where he was

born, but the sign reading *Center of the World* is still there, under the name of his village, Giavenale. I swore I'd write to the mayor, to ask him where this claim to be the epicenter of the planet comes from, if there are geographical reasons I'm unaware of, some prime meridian that passes through the fields of eggplant and squash, like London's Greenwich Meridian, or whether it was a joke made by the village idiot so absurd that everyone thought it must be true.

But I never wrote the mayor. Maybe I'd rather not know.

Maybe Giavenale is not the center of the world; my father, however, was the center of mine.

My paternal grandmother raised silkworms in her house, which she would slip under her robe on winter evenings so that they would not catch cold. My grandfather was a "bovaro," a name that refers to cow herding and to the Bernese mountain dog that normally performs the job. But it was my grandfather who slept like a dog in one of the owner's stables so that the cows wouldn't get loose.

Family lore—and I mean *lore,* because I find it hard to believe that this was the childhood of the man who brought me into this world, his poverty is so far from the comfort with which I grew up that it doesn't seem to have anything to do with me—includes a brother who was a shepherd and an aunt who had lost a leg to a scythe and replaced it with the wooden handle of a broom. Then there was the pig they raised in their courtyard, Christmases when they had nothing but a mandarin to celebrate with, the summers he sold produce at the local markets, starting when he was nine. My father wasn't alone; the entire postwar generation in Italy walked barefoot to primary school.

Years ago, at a film festival, I saw Ermanno Olmi's *The Tree of Wooden Clogs*, winner of the Palme d'Or in 1978. I wept at the extreme poverty of the film's protagonists and their exhausting efforts to survive in a Lombard farmhouse at the end of the nineteenth century. "Dad, you come from the tree of wooden clogs," I told him, stunned myself, as if to prove to him that I had finally understood.

That expression, "the tree of wooden clogs," had long been part of the private language that only the two of us spoke and that has died with him.

Two generations later, the granddaughter and daughter of such people is enjoying a privilege that has never been granted to anyone before: a night alone in the Acropolis Museum.

For the larvae and oxen of her grandparents, she has substituted the marbles of Phidias.

Instead of an impoverished Venetian village convinced it's the center of the planet, she has chosen the genuine navel of the world: Athens.

Barefoot by choice, brazen, under her feet Caryatids separated by a clear glass floor, not the stabbing stones of a dirt road that leads to open fields.

It took me years to admit it, to not insult them and their poverty with my classist shame: these were my people.

* * *

To further "the progress of the Fine Arts in Great Britain." To bestow "some benefit on the progress of taste in England." To improve "the circumstances towards the advancement of literature and the arts." That's what Lord Elgin wrote with conviction to explain the purpose of his Eastern embassy.

So, in the beginning, it was not a question of raiding Greece or filching things from the country, not the smallest stone that we all slip into our pockets along with a seashell for a souvenir (even Chateaubriand, one of Elgin's fiercest detractors, snatched one up from the Parthenon). The English ambassador's intentions were completely artistic in nature, to be carried out exclusively with sketches and casts that he would then send to the museums and art schools of his native country. The idea of excavating or purloining ancient art is never mentioned in the official documents that concern Lord Elgin's embassy in Constantinople.

I believe my father's goal was identical, innocent, and just as visionary: starting from scratch, to improve and advance his family's cultural fate and intellectual prowess.

That man, who in the course of his life had never read a book, not even my own books once I made my stubborn decision to write them, insisted that his daughter possess superior literary taste to him, he who possessed none.

"Study," my father told me as soon I knew the word. He wanted his daughter to speak not only standard Italian but other languages too. If he had had his way, I would have learned every language ever spoken on the planet since the fall of the Tower of Babel.

He called ancient Greek, whose alphabet he didn't understand, "a weirdly written language, like hieroglyphs." Yet it was my father who insisted that as a young girl I attend a *liceo classico* and study ancient languages in a world that peddled the poison of utility as the one and only metric of an education.

He never understood what I did, what I wrote. The long afternoons spent studying in my room troubled him, he who had never sat down at a desk. My teachers intimidated him, so he preferred not to meet them.

Of my scholastic career, which he pretended to understand, as if rather than sell fruit at the market he too had gone to school, he was always pleased, with that indestructible pride typical of the uneducated, who can believe anything unfamiliar to them is a masterpiece.

"You're the one who went to the elite schools," he'd often shrug after I'd had fun humiliating him by making a show of how much better educated I was than him, the son of a cowherd.

I feel ashamed of the superficial know-it-all I once was as I stand before a fragment of the western pediment of the Parthenon: the headless statue of "the dew goddess" Pandrosos embracing her elderly father, Kekrops, the first king of Athens.

I wish I was lucky enough to be able to perform that same gesture once more.

Tonight my arms hold nothing but regret.

I know that if I'm here now, an orphan kneeling at the Acropolis, it's only thanks to my father.

* * *

They had Shakespeare, Swift, and Defoe, yet the English of the nineteenth century still felt they were provincials compared to the ancient Greeks.

I may very well be the most provincial person around, but I don't think there has ever been a human being born after the golden age of Pericles, Phidias, Plato, and Sophocles who didn't feel like a vulgarian compared to classical Athens.

Even on today's Greeks, the effect that ancient Greece has is more like that of the moon than that of the sun: it instills in you a vague restlessness, like when you go on looking for something you've lost despite knowing you'll never find it.

Such unhappiness springs from the grandeur of ancient Greece, which is impossible to forget, impossible to surpass.

This sense of charlatanism has plagued us for over twenty-three centuries, ever since Alexander the Great, a Macedonian, was tutored by Aristotle, a Greek. And even when, during the long centuries of the Middle Ages, knowledge of ancient Greek was lost, Greek art and literature didn't stop being considered the pinnacle of human wisdom, worth transmitting by hand with the persistence and patience of legions of monks.

It's impossible not to feel inadequate and flawed before the immensity of the classical world, the mirror and magnet of our incompleteness. From the Renaissance to the Baroque period, we had at least merely limited ourselves to copying from Greece, like dull and lazy pupils who, taking a test, hope to save themselves from their own mediocrity by copying from the best kid in class.

The nineteenth century of Elgin, Fauvel, Choiseul-Gouffier, and everyone who returned to Western Europe with a piece of Greece in their pocket marked a passage in the history of our inferiority complex toward the classics that we cannot rectify, when the cheater suddenly turned into the thief.

It was no longer enough to send the wealthiest scions on educational trips to Athens and the most brilliant minds on world tours, as had begun to happen in the eighteenth century, taking up a custom of the ancient Romans: to enhance the aesthetic taste and intellectual depth of Europe it was necessary to abscond with the very idea of Greece, as if it were our own. As if it were Helen of Sparta spirited away to Troy, or the Elgin Marbles to London.

And ever since, the ignorant student has pretended to be the know-it-all professor.

Curled up on the cold floor in a corner of the museum, I think I understand how the first man expelled from Eden must have felt.

My head is almost spinning from all the intensity. I have the impression I can feel the physical heft of the bodies that sculpted these marbles day after day, the muscular arms that hammered away at the delicate stone, their large fingers gripping the chisel, the drops of sweat wrung by the Greek sun that fell into the pores of the sculptures in front of me.

When faced with an immortal work of art, be it in Athens or at the Louvre or the Uffizi, I often think of the mortality of the person who made it, of all the devotion and care as well as the boredom needed to write, to paint, to sculpt.

To live.

In the pen, brush, and chisel, I have a strong sense of the death of those who held them in their hands. And then I regret my lack of faith.

Tonight, more than dead bodies, what torments me are the souls of those people who placed the Acropolis atop the world forever.

In no other place in the world does one so easily, so serenely abandon reality for dreams. In Greece the extraordinary always emerges in the form of a miracle out of the need for myth.

The first marble to make up part of the Elgin collection seems to obey the laws of fate. Or the first page of a Greek literature textbook.

Because the ambassador had yet to set foot on Hellas' sacred turf when the immense classical world appeared to him and beckoned him to encounter Homer.

Elgin was still aboard the HMS Phaeton and bound for Turkey when chance steered him to no less a place than Troy.

At the Dardanelles, the Elgins were invited aboard the Sultan Selim, the flagship of the Turkish fleet helmed by the Pasha captain. This was their first encounter with the magnificence and lavishness of the Turks, which made their jaws drop. The ship's cabins glittered with gold and silk, bejeweled sabers hung on the walls like paintings. Dinner was served on a dish made of Dresden porcelain and coffee in diamond cups that reflected the light cast by slender Japanese lamps. After supper came gifts: Elgin was presented with twenty-five rams and six oxen, but above all with gold, diamonds, rubies, emeralds, and endless skeins of precious fabrics.

Resuming their journey, still dizzy from this first taste of sumptuous Turkish customs, the English ambassador was forced to put in at the island of Tenedos (Bozcaada in Turkish) due to contrary winds. Clutching their copies of the *Iliad*, the English travelers decided to make the most of their involuntary stopover and explore the Trojan plain.

It is Lady Elgin, in a letter sent to her mother, who describes that incredible day at the home of Hector and Priam. Before complaining about the hardships of the long journey, she writes:

> We took guides and off we set to the supposed site of ancient Troy; we rode ten miles across the plain, saw camels grazing, and arrived at a romantic spot where they shewed us the ruins of the outside walls. And compleat ruins it is, for there are not two stones left one upon another only it is visible there has been a great quantity of building. The Learned Men had taken Homer with them, and from examining the spot they agreed there was every appearance of its being the place.

It was during this expedition to Troy, with Homer as guide, that Elgin saw two ancient monuments known to the first explorer-archaeologists of the eighteenth century and which many had already tried to remove and transfer to Europe, but never succeeded. They were two marble slabs, one decorated with a bas-relief depicting some mothers in the company of their children, and the other bearing a very ancient inscription in Greek written first from right to left and then again left to right. This style of writing is called boustrophedon, or turn-like, the way oxen turn while plowing.

The reasons the inhabitants of the remote Turkish village had always refused to sell the marbles to the many English and French travelers willing to pay their weight in gold had nothing to do with the artistic value of the monuments. In one of those spectacular fusions of paganism and Christianity only found in

Greece, where the sun is a sort of shaker that makes an intoxicating cocktail of Hellenic enchantment, the priests of the village church told Elgin that those two stones were an infallible cure-all.

The English ambassador probably kept his composure as he listened to the priests' explanations, just as we might feign to listen to people who question the basic principles of science or democracy today. And with the same resolve, a moment later he must have laid claim to the two slabs, an action the pasha readily authorized; a sovereign who offers his guests diamonds could hardly refuse him a few chunks of chipped stone valuable only in the eyes of superstitious Greek infidels.

A few days later, the two slabs were torn from the village where they had been worshipped for thousands of years and crammed into the hold of a ship bound for London, amid the tears of the villagers and the curses of the priests. Apparently, the curses worked, since the ship sank at the mouth of the Thames, just outside London, and her cargo was lost forever.

Thus began the story of Lord Elgin's collection, with a shipwreck and a hex on the Trojan plain. The sea decided to swallow up what had been wrongfully taken from Greece. However, this first Homeric punishment was nothing compared to the curse of Minerva who, with the patience of adversity, waited for the ambassador to arrive in Athens.

* * *

Elgin and his wife landed in Constantinople in November 1799, two months after setting sail from Portsmouth. The reception given them by the grand vizier's officials was so spectacular as to make them believe that the gifts received by the pasha at the Dardanelles were but a foretaste of the Turkish luxuries that they would enjoy in the years to come. For almost two weeks Elgin was showered with welcoming gifts from officers of every corps and military rank and he was driven through the narrow streets of Constantinople on gilded chariots escorted by dozens of servants. But that was just the tip of the iceberg: the actual inauguration ceremony would take place in the palace of the sultan himself, where hundreds of guests were served a thirty-six-course dinner on silver platters. Being a woman, Lady Elgin could not enter the sultan's court, but the young bride had no intention of missing out on the main spectacle of that world, which must have seemed to her to be the Elysian Fields of gold and diamonds. So she got herself on the guest list as Lord Bruce and showed up at the dinner disguised as a young gentleman.

It was thanks to the international situation, which saw England newly allied with Turkey against the threat of Bonaparte, that Elgin's embassy enjoyed a treatment à la *The Arabian Nights*. For his part, Napoleon wrote next to Elgin's name in his correspondence "*un des plus grands ennemis de la nation.*" If the ire of a great historical figure can occasionally be flattering, it didn't do the English ambassador any favors, for he would pay dearly for the emperor's hatred of him.

On the other side of the Aegean Sea, the artists hired by Elgin arrived in Athens in the summer of 1800. To them went the task of carrying out the work on which the fate of Great Britain's artistic taste depended.

The head of the crew was a then well-known Italian painter, Giovanni Battista Lusieri, who had already been commissioned by the King of Naples to draw the ancient monuments of Sicily and Magna Graecia. Elgin met him during a stopover in Taormina during the HMS Phaeton's long crossing to Constantinople and immediately hired him. The contract was supposed to last for the duration of the embassy; neither had any idea that it would blossom into a genuine friendship that would endure over twenty years, arguably the one reliable attachment Elgin would form in the name of Greece.

Athens was then a city on the periphery of Europe, dirty and miserable, with no trace of its past greatness, neglected by time and its inhabitants. It counted no more than thirteen hundred houses, all occupied by a poor population that came from every region of the Ottoman Empire. At the time, only half of Athens' inhabitants were Greek, a quarter were Turkish, and the rest were Balkan, Jewish, Italian, and North African.

As for its administration, the city was governed by two officials who took their orders directly from the sultan of Constantinople, the voivode, who performed the role of governor, and a fortress commander known as the dizdar. However humiliating to the Greeks, their rule was not tyrannical, and the different nationalities coexisted peacefully and frequently intermarried.

The Acropolis retained only one thing from the classical era: its name. Over the centuries the Turkish garrison had transformed it into a kind of unsanitary slum where shacks were swept away with every storm.

At the time, the contrast of the magnificence of its ancient monuments and the poverty of Athens must have been striking. In the middle of hovels stood the lofty Parthenon, the Erechtheion, the Propylaea and, in the low-lying area of the city, the temple of Hephaestus. Hidden, abandoned, the remains of later monuments, such as the Tower of the Winds, the monument of Lysicrates, and some gigantic columns belonging to the ancient temple of Zeus, weathered time and forgetfulness.

Since the ancient buildings were the only solid constructions in all of Athens, they had been quickly repurposed with neither archaeological scruple nor a sense of guilt. The Erechtheion was converted into a powder keg, the temple of Hephaestus into a church, the Tower of the Winds into the headquarters of dervishes. The Parthenon was now reduced to a mosque equipped with cannons to ward off enemies. The Turks were reckless with the ruins, planting their gardens between steles and recycling older monuments for building material. Classical sculptures were placed on the roofs of modern houses, like talismans of a lost era.

What is stunning is not so much that, just two centuries ago, goats peacefully grazed among the rubbish and gunpowder around the Parthenon that tonight I've been called on to guard. No, what is surprising is the fact that, after two thousand five hundred years and a history of neglect and oblivion, the Parthenon is still standing.

Shortly after my arrival this evening, while waiting for the night watchmen to start their shift, I forced myself to rewatch the Acropolis Museum's short introductory video for visitors before they go out to see what remains in Athens of the marbles of Phidias. I must have seen it at least a dozen times over the years, I almost know by heart the English voiceover that narrates how the Parthenon has been desecrated through the ages.

Every time I watch it I feel upset, violated, as if the classical world had been raped. Over time, the columns of the temple of Athena, originally red and blue, not the austere white we think of today, lost their color. More significantly, the Parthenon lost the respect of people who would pass it on to posterity.

The Romans and Byzantines robbed Athens of its statues, the Visigoths of Alaric sacked every corner of the city, but up until then no one had dared touch the buildings of the Acropolis. The first crack of the whip and blow of the pick occurred in the fifth century AD, a thousand years after Phidias created the work, with the advent of Christianity, which constrained the Parthenon to bend to its new religion and converted it into a church. The eastern flank was gutted to make room for an apse and windows were installed along the sides.

Although the pressure of iconoclasm led to the defacement and destruction of a large number of sculptures, the Parthenon didn't undergo any significant changes for almost another thousand years. Miraculously, Byzantines, Franks, Catalans, Florentines, and Venetians passed through Athens without touching the Acropolis until the Ottoman occupation of Greece. In fact, in the fourteenth century the Turks converted the Parthenon church to a mosque, complete with a crescent moon and minaret, while the Erechtheion, likely given the feminine presence of the Caryatids, became the castle warden's harem.

Before Elgin came along, the worst blow to the Parthenon had been dealt by Venice: in 1687, the Venetian General Francesco Morosini lay siege to the Acropolis and didn't think twice about firing cannons at the Parthenon, then used by the Turks as a gunpowder store. The building lit up like a tinderbox, the original roof was blown to pieces, most of the sculptures were damaged, and deep cracks opened along the colonnade.

Morosini was also the first to presume to take the Parthenon sculptures home to Venice as souvenirs of war. And he was the first to have to contend with the stubbornness of Athena, determined to defend the works of art that had been offered to her. The Venetian ordered his workers to remove the imposing group of sculptures that decorated the western pediment depicting the dispute between Athena and Poseidon for control of Attica, a dispute won by the goddess, who offered the city olive trees.

When the marbles were about to be lowered to the ground, the ropes holding up the precarious scaffolding broke under their weight, and the statues smashed to the ground. Morosini was forced to abandon most of the Parthenon statues in Athens, except for a few fragments and three heads, one of which can now be found in Paris and the other two, for some reason, in chilly Copenhagen. But the rest of the pediment is kept in the British Museum.

The Turks never suspected that the ancient ruins held artistic value. Their attitude towards the classical world was always pragmatic: if an ancient building was solid enough to be recycled, it was readily transformed into a stable or granary; if its materials were judged useful, it was broken up and repurposed. But if a monument simply existed and posed no problems for the Turks, they didn't bother demolishing it and instead granted it the privilege of falling into ruin all on its own.

True, the Turks made no effort to protect the Parthenon, but they did work to ensure that human greed didn't add to the inevitable ravages of time. They never granted anyone official permission to remove even the smallest of statues. That was an ironclad rule that extended all the way to the sultan of Constantinople, and it regularly frustrated the French ambassador Choiseul-Gouffier and his painter Fauvel, who were never authorized to climb up to the Acropolis and were forced to bribe local authorities in order to seize the marbles now housed in the Louvre.

During the eighteenth century, a new, graver threat arrived from Western Europe: so-called "educational" tourism. During the eighteenth century, more and more travelers claiming to be lovers of classical culture flocked to Athens; wealthy Europeans wielding the works of Homer and Plato and, more importantly, the money to pay off local authorities for permission to bring a few Greek souvenirs back to the "civilized" world. Generously remunerated, the Turks began turning one blind eye and then another to the theft of fragments which they didn't recognize as having any value, while still upholding the ban on climbing to the Acropolis.

Savvy businessmen, the Turks soon saw that they could make

a tidy profit by selling small fragments of columns or sculptures, easier to transport than large and onerous finds, to rich and dainty Europeans, and didn't hesitate to split up ancient statues and auction off the fragments to the highest bidder.

The more hardheaded and foolish among them couldn't believe that Westerners were willing to pay a fortune for scraps of old marble and suspected that there were nuggets of gold hidden inside the ancient artifacts. They made no scruples about destroying the artifacts on their hunt for imaginary treasures.

Back home, European tourists quickly lost interest in their old souvenirs and deposited them in some dark corner of their manors to be later tossed out by their heirs, as happened to the Fagan fragment gifted to the Salinas Archaeological Museum by Robert Fagan's widow.

Most of the Parthenon fragments taken from Greece in the eighteenth century have been lost. Over the years, some parts of Phidia's frieze have mysteriously resurfaced in the gardens of an English castle or the display cabinets of wealthy French families. Hard as it is to believe, while I'm spending the night in front of the vacuum left by Western Europe at the Acropolis Museum, someone in France or England may be harboring a fragment of the Parthenon in their living room or forgotten in their cellar.

* * *

The concept of the "classical" is immaterial as ever, it is almost the breath of the world we inhabit today. Like the atmosphere, the classical world animates the air in which our thoughts are formed and of which Antiquity is the pristine oxygen.

Of the classical world, the Acropolis is both a symbol and idea.

What from the start has disturbed me about the Parthenon's fate is not so much the fact that an English ambassador arrived one fine day in the nineteenth century and, amid general indifference, absconded with it.

What disturbs me is that for two thousand years or more, until at least the eighteenth century, no one ever suspected that it had any value worth defending.

I struggle to imagine the men and women who, from ancient Rome to the Middle Ages to the eighteenth century and beyond, lifted their gaze towards the same Acropolis that I now face and saw nothing but a marble quarry, a place to store gunpowder, a supermarket of objects and souvenirs. What curse was lurking under their amnesia?

Had they really felt no awe as they stood before Phidia's work, only the desire to pillage and destroy it? If no one in Rome, Paris, or Venice would ever dare to reach out and steal a fragment of the Sistine Chapel or the Basilica of San Marco, why is it that in Athens it was so damn easy to transform the classical world into a bargain basement bazaar?

Standing in front of the Parthenon marbles tonight, I feel a sense of dread. As with any story, tragic stories especially, I'm afraid it could be repeated, like a nightmare one can't outrun.

If for two millennia it was impossible to recognize the value of Phidia's marbles, the most majestic and impressive remains of the ancient world, with their powdery gray beauty clearly visible above Athens, then I wonder how we can defend the ideas and values of the classical world today. Unlike the Parthenon, those aren't made of stone. They are invisible, impalpable. Grand yet fragile.

I have the impression that, in the story of our current obliviousness and ingratitude that we're all writing (and that future generations will read the same way that I'm retracing the story of Elgin), the role of naive and gullible Turks, too ignorant to see that the classical world held value, is our own.

Every time we normalize the question "What purpose do the classics serve?" and ignore the fact that only servants "serve," whereas culture is liberating, we are blinding ourselves. Beset by the same cataracts that afflicted those who, only a couple of centuries ago, saw nothing in the Acropolis but old marble to be broken into pieces.

In the eighteenth century it was easy for thieves to steal a few stones from incompetent and ill-informed people willing to smash ancient works for a handful of coins. Conformity and the market logic that we apply to education today suggest that we're the same, passively relinquishing the classical world—and not out of premeditated greed but puerile ignorance.

Like immature children, or beggars turned greedy by a system that operates on the profit motive, we'll gladly give up priceless treasures in exchange for a piece of candy.

And yet the classics are the most important thing we own. The very stuff of our soul.

By putting them up for sale, we wander through life unable to articulate thought, with our heads cut off, like the statues of the Parthenon.

I look with horror at a metope that shows a Centaur gripping the throat of a Lapith, as if trying to crush it.

In my chest I feel the same ancestral grip.

I think to myself that eternity isn't like the work of Phidias, it isn't made of marble. It is contained in each passing moment: get distracted for a second, stop watching over it, and it'll be lost forever.

Italy returned everything. Paris, Copenhagen, Würzburg, Karlsruhe and, of course, London are the cities where to this day the groaning fragments of the Parthenon stolen from Greece still lie.

I promise myself that after my one night at the Acropolis Museum I'll visit every place in the world where what was stolen from Athens is kept.

A pilgrimage. Or a penance rather.

To atone for this history of treating with recklessness every fragment of marble behind which the severe, sacred, mysterious face of Athena looms.

Night spreads its shadow over Athens, the chariot of the Sun is far gone.

I'd give anything to be able to smoke a cigarette, even if I act like I quit a few years ago. Packs of Hellas Specials, an old brand of cigarettes, once featured the Acropolis at night lit by a full, round moon, like a vinyl record. Stop thinking about it, I tell myself: I'm not going to be the failed Hellenist forced to write on her résumé that she set fire to the Phidias marbles just because she wanted a smoke.

Besides, I have a date tonight.

Not only with the classical world and my conscience, I mean.

I have a date with the recipient of the postcard I bought before coming here.

He's the one I asked to pass by the windows of the museum at the stroke of midnight.

To give visitors a sense of the shape and scope of what is missing, the Acropolis museum decided to leave the gaps exposed.

The room in which I have set up my cot is the exact size of the Parthenon frieze, which, unfurled like a fine ribbon made of marble, measures about one hundred and sixty meters. Arranged in this imaginary rectangle are all ninety-two metopes of the school of Phidias, including those lost over time. More importantly, including those currently held hostage at the British Museum.

For the approximately thirty meters of marble relegated to

oblivion, of which today no fragment remains, not even the dust of memory, the museum has chosen to keep the corresponding panel empty. The effect is that of an enormous collection of stamps in which some squares remain empty, the letters mailed but never arrived, leaving the visitor to imagine shapes and colors that they will never see.

Where, thanks to sketches made by traveling artists in the seventeenth and eighteenth centuries, we can at least picture what the lost sculptures looked like, a black and white reproduction has been placed in the corner of the empty panel, so the visitor can intuit what they are being compelled to feel nostalgic about.

The fifty or so meters currently in London are, here at the Acropolis Museum, a kind of shrill, chalk-white color. In order not to avoid interruptions to Phidia's story, the missing metopes have been replaced by plaster casts (temporarily, so the Greeks never tire of hoping). This way, a visitor can still hear the rustling of women's tunics as they march on Athena's feast day, the lowing of sacrificed oxen, the straining of men's muscles under the weight of gifts without stumbling over every absence and desecration.

Most of all, the viewer can more readily absorb the horror of the Centauromachy, the ancestral struggle between the rational and irrational carved into the metopes on the southern end, and puzzle over which side to take, that of humans or that of beasts.

In front of me, a Pentelic marble foot, yellowed by time and rain, has been set in a bright white plaster block. It's illuminated by museum lights. Tonight it looks more like a decayed tooth in a dental impression than an immortal stone.

An arm, two legs, an entire body appear in succession and then again absence absence absence, as if Phidia's frieze were bent on using empty and filled-in spaces to create a kind of Morse code of European civilization—and its greed.

* * *

The waning moon sits high and incomplete in the sky above Mount Lycabettus. It's almost time for my appointment, in view of which I feel the same excitement and dread as when I was twenty.

The series of marble and plaster sculptures beside me make me think of the Stations of the Cross. I wonder, then, where the final sacrifice will take place and whether I'll be the one sacrificed.

And whether somewhere there'll be a resurrection, or whether such a possibility has been lost like the bas-reliefs of Phidias, of which there remains not even a pencil sketch in the notebook of the last human being to have seen them with their own eyes.

I should buy some plaster and spread it on my soul, I think, looking at the impassive expression on a handmaid's face, hardened by the wind and pasted onto her artificial body. I should strut through the streets of life with my head held high, as if it were a feast day in ancient Athens.

Yet the fiercer part of me can't resist the gash, the slap in the face. It has known ceasefires, but never peace.

I don't think it will ever be appeased. I'm sick of coming to terms with the holes left behind by wounds. I don't have time for them to scar over anymore, I realize, peevish and keen to exact reparations, as if life were just a matter of debts to be paid and credits to be claimed.

Surely it's just my craving for a cigarette, but I feel welling up inside me the need to judge, the need to console myself by organizing the history of the Parthenon marbles into good and evil, victim and perpetrator.

And for the first time I'm seized by a furious desire to go to London and bring the lost marbles back to Athens.

Before this evening, I'd never had that kind of thought.

I'd never really lost my cool over the endless injustice done to Greece, a country that for centuries has been reduced to a bargain bin of art and ideas where every tourist—otherwise shy and reserved in, say, Paris or London or Berlin—starts noisily haggling over prices.

At most I might heave a superficial sigh over Elgin's fraud, like someone who one minute feigns to be disturbed by scenes of disaster glimpsed from the comfort of their couch and the next minute is giddily booking a weekend in London to see statues that are Athens' by birthright.

A violent urge seizes me as I face the chipped and reassembled metopes like a stone puzzle, disabusing me of any Zen proverb about acceptance and truces.

Of course I'd end up in prison. They'd compare me to the crazy woman at the British Museum who slipped a Phidias marble into her purse and planned to bring it back to Athens. At the very least they'd think it was some stunt, like the one a few weeks ago at the Louvre when a guy threw a piece of cake at the Mona Lisa to remind this comatose world of the climate crisis. International lawsuits would be brought against me, a coward, more afraid of judges and courts than hospitals.

I'd soon find myself—now I'm daydreaming—in all the newspapers of the world with a blurry photo and underneath it a caption applauding me for being the biggest champion of Greek culture, philhellene of the philhellenes. Never imagining I'd been drawn to the theft of Lord Elgin, they'd call me the new Lord Byron, willing to die to defend Greece's honor. After a few days, I'd have earned the epithet of *héroïne grecque* that *Le Monde* prematurely bestowed on me. It would become my calling card, maybe my next tattoo.

I'd carry on my deception undaunted, and it would get bigger and bigger and go unpunished. I'd receive prizes and honors, maybe even honorary Greek citizenship, who knows. And although I'd still need an interpreter to deliver my solemn speeches in modern Greek and thank the ever-growing and devoted public for me, no one would know that I'd been motivated not by some Homeric ardor but by laziness.

By tiredness.

By my inability to accept imperfection, an ability the stones in the Acropolis Museum themselves possess, having carried on after the catastrophe with patience and dignity.

For a moment I abandon myself to my dream of plaster and deceit, imagining this museum finally filled to bursting, all the marbles of Phidias back where they should be: hands reattached to arms; knights astride their beautiful horses; heads, once scattered around the world, finally connected to their bodies again.

And so it would be for all the museums of Greece, their Victories and Venuses once again towering above the sea of Samothrace, Milos, and the various other islands, deposited back on the pedestals on which they had once been carefully set by ancient sculptors and venerated by hordes of modern tourists.

I let myself be carried away by the image of a Greece finally acknowledged and repaired. And more than justly repaid. If every reader of Homer, beginning two thousand eight hundred years ago, when the muse on Helicon sang the deeds of Achilles and Odysseus to the blind man of Chios, had paid Greece even a fraction of a typical copyright fee, this handful of barren islands that the gods tossed like dice into the Aegean Sea would now be the lushest, most prosperous country in the world.

Far more than oil, gas, or any other natural resources snatched from the earth in morsels, the intellectual resources that since its foundation Greece has offered to world civilization represent a heritage of inestimable value and hard for the rest of the planet to compensate.

Were every man and woman who ever had an idea after reading Plato or Aristotle, who ever exclaimed "Eureka!" after studying Archimedes or Eratosthenes, who ever felt the urge to write, paint, and play music after attending a tragedy by Sophocles—or simply felt better understood, less flawed and more humane—to turn around and acknowledge their debt to the Classics, Greece would be sitting atop the world—atop Olympus!—revered and respected by every other country that humbly begged at the foot of its grandeur.

* * *

Finally my fit of madness passes, I stop fantasizing about being the savior of Greece and a trafficker of modern art.

Who asked me to be, anyways? Who entrusted me with such a task?

Sometimes I have the unsettling suspicion that my rage for the classics stems more from pride than love.

For a moment I succumbed to the weakness of assembling courts and partitioning blame. It's so reassuring to pretend you're on the right side and blame others for the crushing pain in your chest.

It's comforting, but I know it serves no purpose.

Yet tonight I no longer feel like working on any missing pieces I may have, on the contrary I want to feel that the gaps are narrower and more solid than Phidia's marbles, which, disfigured or not, seem more presentable than me.

I want to believe for a moment that it is possible to go back to being intact, to being whole, even if I have to sit on the floor and glue the pieces of the Parthenon together with my own two hands.

* * *

In less than a minute it'll be midnight. I'm ready.

I'm barefoot. My red toenails scurry across the cold floor, like insects.

Upright as a soldier, I stand beside the magnificent akroterion, the flower or palm-like decoration that crowned the roof of the Parthenon. Drawn to the drama of the frieze, I'd never noticed how beautiful it was, over four meters high, with its sinuous and regal volutes placed at the top of the pediment like a plume on a parade hat.

I'm sure he'll come.
But I'm afraid he won't come.
That he'll simply change his mind as he's walking along the cobbled street leading him, on a night at the end of May, to the foot of the Acropolis to meet a woman shut inside a museum and surrounded by ruins.
For me this man is the image of life itself.
Every day I need physical proof of his existence, as if to take the pulse of my own.
Otherwise I wouldn't believe it.

Suddenly, the lights of the museum go out one by one, giving way to a very ancient sleep that leaves me completely in the dark in front of the Acropolis, forever lit like a lighthouse.

Then I feel panic mount, not for the chance of my stumbling in the dark on a Parthenon marble, but for the possibility that this man, once he arrives, won't be able to see me and therefore will go elsewhere, to look for someone less complicated, less intense than me.

Outside the window, the streetlights dimly illuminate the road of Dionysius the Areopagite, even if by now there is no one traveling it. The few passersby carrying beers who, as carefree as a late spring evening, crossed it a few hours ago will clearly have gone home by now, to sleep or make love.

*

Then I see him. My man.

I love picking his profile out of a crowd, it's like hearing a familiar sounding word in a foreign language.

Punctual as the lighting system, at midnight he waves at me under the windows of the Acropolis Museum.

He can't see me, despite my gesticulating to drive out the punishing dark that now engulfs me. His belief in my presence is an act of faith, he doesn't move an inch.

But I see him and that's enough confirmation for me that tonight this man still exists.

Just as the bodies of everyone in Athens who loved one another existed before us and how the bodies of everyone who will love each other after us will exist, long after we've disintegrated in the earth, us and our sighs, at the foot of the Acropolis.

The pen, that chatterbox, as Zorba the Greek would say. Sometimes, it's a machine of misapprehensions, of misunderstandings. Of deceit.

Lord Elgin was still getting used to the calm sun and lazy waters of the Bosphorus when he suddenly and undeservedly found himself the most prominent man in all Constantinople. The success of the English expedition to Egypt and Napoleon's retreat made the ambassador, who had contributed quite little to those outcomes, the darling of the sultan's court.

The Turks, ecstatic at the idea of being able to take back the land of the Pharaohs from the French, never stopped to display their gratitude with feasts and gifts to the country that had restored to the empire its honor and one of its provinces. When the news of victory was announced in Constantinople, the sultan called for seven days of celebrations throughout the city, with music and dancing on every street corner, fireworks lighting up both banks of the Bosphorus, and cannons fired through the night.

Elgin and his diplomats were clearly delighted by this unexpected reversal of fortune in their favor. "I think they might have conquered Egypt over and over again had they but fired half the number of cannon in earnest they are now firing in joke," a pleased Lady Elgin wrote to her mother.

But the ambassador had no intention of settling for the usual gala suppers, diamonds, and fine fabrics.

Elgin wanted more. He wanted the Acropolis of Athens. That was his initial project, which had always been denied the French and, of all the Turks' gifts, had become for him a point of honor.

He didn't have to wait long, that's for sure: the firman, the official permit that allowed Lusieri and the other workers in Elgin's employ to go up to the Acropolis, arrived less than three weeks after the English victory in Egypt. For the sultan, it was a minor concession, a modest addition to the long list of furs, horses, medals, and precious stones with which he was generously showing his gratitude to his British allies.

More precisely, the firman is an official letter signed by a minister of the sultan and addressed to the voivode (military leader) and the prefect of Athens. Like all bureaucratic documents, it is written in a solemn, convoluted, and obscure style, more like the writing of a seventeenth-century country notary than the rigorous and open prose of Plato. Although it appeared to be thorough and meticulous, Elgin's firman contains a carefully calculated ambiguity at a crucial point in the text: the passage that permitted the English to take possession of the Parthenon frieze.

The ambassador's requests are reeled off with total precision: he expects his artists to have free entry to the Acropolis and make sketches and casts without anyone hampering their projects; the right to erect scaffolding for their research and to dig for new finds without encountering obstacles; above all, he demands that there be no *"opposizione al portar via qualche pezzo di pietra con vecchie inscrizioni o sculture,"* i.e., no opposition to their taking away pieces of stone with old figures or inscriptions.

I can't help but gasp when I come across the cheerful music of Italian syllables in the Elgin archives. Like nice weather, they penetrate the foggy sounds of English and British accents. It's the same melody my vocal cords learned to reproduce as a hallmark of my homeland: *Italia*. The same intonation that injects a Mediterranean lilt into every other language I speak.

But, in a sadistic twist of fate, the only remaining copy of the pickaxe that the British used to ransack Athens is written in my native tongue. A few words in Italian are enough to make me feel even more guilty for brazenly wielding Elgin's biography in front of the mutilated and beheaded Parthenon marbles. As if I were responsible for the language that I think in, that I write in.

Despite all the historical research that has been conducted in the archives across Europe, the original Turkish version has been lost, as have the ambassador's notes in English. The only attestation of the firman that would have authorized Elgin to transport the marbles of the Parthenon to London, the one he himself would exhibit in court twenty years later to defend himself against the infamous accusation of theft, is an Italian version produced by a man named Pisani, the interpreter of the British Embassy in Constantinople.

The first blow to the Parthenon consists of a few decisive words, tacked onto the end of the document, maybe at the last minute, clearly with the intention of making it look to the prefect of Athens as if after all the more substantial requests it were a minor detail to grant them permission to carry off the works of art that had jutted from the Acropolis for two millennia.

In relation to those "pieces of stone," the firman proceeds confusingly, reformulating and inverting the terms of that same fateful sentence. You don't need a lawyer to see that the document is vague: authorizing someone to "dig and take" is not the same as consenting to "take and dig." The former clearly establishes the right to take away only those works that emerge from their excavation campaigns. The latter grants permission to remove any valuable object whatsoever, regardless of where it is found, whether under the sacred ground of Athens or directly on the metopes and pediments of the Parthenon. And it's here that the postil turns elusive.

To judge someone based on what you believe they intended to do and not on what they actually did: courts don't allow us to put intentions on trial, much less the memory of an entire people. Our conscience, on the other hand, sometimes does.

If we wanted to put Lord Elgin's motives on trial today, we'd have to recognize that, in the beginning, the ambassador hadn't even noticed the extraordinary impunity granted to the British by the firman.

Elgin doesn't hide his enthusiasm and satisfaction in any of his letters after the signing of the official document by the pasha. He always speaks of casts, copies, drawings, even archaeological digs and research into the foundations of the Acropolis, never of looting and theft. His interpretation of the firman was initially restrictive and respectful of the limits imposed by the Greek authorities, and by a crumb of conscience.

Originally the ambassador hadn't contemplated placing his hand and knife-edge on the friezes of the Parthenon to take them away. His sole purpose was to create casts and drawings that, once shown to the educated public, would contribute to the development of fine arts and letters in England. But as soon as he was given permission, he realized that the original is always better than the copy. Why send a plaster frieze to England when he could send Phidia's Pentelic marble itself?

So, if Elgin didn't intend to remove the stones—an idea that appears not to have occurred to him—then why are the marbles, which Phidias sculpted with patience and genius twenty-five centuries ago, now in London and no longer above Athens, where they had been placed by Pericles and the Olympians?

The ancient Greeks would have called it *tyche*: a question of luck, the will of fate.

We might call it destiny, though we can't honestly say that things had to go this way, because it is *unacceptable* that they happened exactly this way.

I hate it when humans resign themselves to fate; it strikes me as bordering on inanition, or cowardice.

Because it may be true that what happens to us is out of our control, but our freedom to choose how to react to what happens to us remains inviolable.

More than by Lord Elgin and his firman, the Parthenon should have been shielded against the whims of fate.

The same, inexplicable fate that, almost unwillingly, brought me face to face with these broken marbles one night at the end of May.

* * *

The future is a word that attests to the absence of the present.

It's easy, childish even, to judge yesterday with the wisdom of today when the wisdom of today will become tomorrow's ignorance. Hindsight generates regrets and accusations, never justice and healing.

In the history of Elgin's responsibility and how the marbles ended up in London, the dance of fortuity almost makes one smile for the carelessness with which it unfolded until the time came to pick up the chisels and hacksaws and break apart the Parthenon.

The source of it all was Napoleon, the force behind every whim of the matter. Had the emperor not lost the campaign in Egypt, there is no doubt that the Turks wouldn't have been so generous and open to an English ambassador with a taste for antiquing. In all likelihood, the sultan wouldn't have thought twice about denying Elgin's request to climb up to the Acropolis, as he had already done several times in the past, and no doctored firman would have reached the prefect of Athens.

And there is *almost* no doubt that, had Napoleon triumphed in Egypt against Turkey and England, every last speck of Phidia's frieze would now be on display at the Louvre. Rather than an Egyptian obelisk, the whole Parthenon might be looming above Paris!

The second most fateful turn of events involves the appropriately named Philip Hunt, chaplain of the Elgin embassy, who throughout the episode was always in the right place at the right time—and with the wrong intentions.

In 1801 Hunt traveled to Athens several times on matters of business and because he had a certain amateurish interest in the ancient world. Thanks to his knowledge of the city, he gained Elgin's trust; Elgin considered him more of a secretary given his business in Greece than a religious man given his spiritual spasms.

In Constantinople it may have been Hunt who drew up the first draft of the firman, with the notes in Italian on the original document, and the clergyman was probably the one who inserted the last ambiguous footnote, too. And it was again Hunt whom Elgin asked to bring the firman to Athens and present it to the Greek authorities, a mission which the clergyman carried out with high hopes and plenty of zeal.

Hunt left Constantinople for Athens in July 1801. In addition to the firman, he carried in his suitcase all kinds of documents to ensure he'd be warmly received by the Greek administration, as well as the expected jewelry, fabrics, and gifts. Having survived a pirate attack—a routine affair at the time—his ship docked at the port of Piraeus on July 22. In the meantime, Elgin's workers, led by the painter Lusieri, had managed to climb the Acropolis a couple of times, but at a steep toll: the extortions and interruptions of Turkish soldiers thwarted their search attempts.

Having learned that the English artists were being blackmailed, Reverend Hunt showed very little reverence for the prefect of Athens at his reception. He flew into a rage at the treatment of Elgin's emissaries and demanded that all the English be granted access to the Acropolis.

When the confused Greek authorities, who couldn't believe the veracity of the firman and all that it implied, protested, Hunt lost his temper again and threatened to exile anyone who opposed the will of the padishah of Constantinople and Her Majesty's ambassador.

After a series of heated exchanges between the increasingly furious reverend and the increasingly terrified Greeks, and after the negotiating table was laden with a slew of precious gifts, Hunt could finally bask in his triumph: the Acropolis would be opened from dawn to dusk to all English citizens, and Elgin's artists could set about their work protected and undisturbed.

What later took possession of the reverend may have been delusions of omnipotence, as often happens to subordinates who, due to completely fortuitous circumstances, find themselves wielding an ounce of power and a bit of spending money.

In the days that followed, Hunt hurried like a hyena to feed upon the privileges that the firman granted to the English. He hired a team of Greeks and ordered them to strip the Acropolis of any stone bearing an inscription, and those stones were immediately put on a ship docked at Piraeus. New excavation campaigns were inaugurated on the Acropolis and the portico of the Caryatids was liberated from its oppressive modern walls.

Finally, in this tale of authorizations and scraps of paper, an increasingly ambitious and hungry Hunt took the step—the decisive bite—of forwarding his official request to the prefect to remove the most perfect metope adorning the Parthenon.

At first the officer hesitated, but the reverend attempted

to convince him with his usual combination of threats and gifts. Meanwhile, the prefect of Athens had died and his son hoped to succeed him, perhaps counting on a recommendation from Lord Elgin to the sultan of Constantinople; therefore, no one objected to Hunt's outrageous demands. Only Spiridon Logothetis, a British consul of Greek nationality, opposed the imminent looting of the Acropolis, but Hunt convinced him that refusing the will of his direct superior, Ambassador Elgin, was not a good idea.

The prefect of Athens, terrified and timid, was thus led to believe that the firman delivered by the British actually authorized them to plunder the Parthenon, carrying off works that time and multiple invasions had spared. Official permission was at last granted.

And that is how Elgin's workers began to dismember the temple of Athena Parthenos with the steady hand of a butcher preparing the best cuts of meat for someone's dinner party.

Fifteen years on, during the investigations of the London commission into whether Elgin's work ought to be considered theft, Hunt was asked if the Greek authorities had realized that by granting him permission to forcibly remove the works of Phidias they were exceeding the legal bounds established by the firman. Not to mention the moral bounds of all Greece.

Hunt responded with a shrug and a nod: yes.

As if to imply that if the Greeks now found themselves divested of the marbles, it was their own arbitrary decisions to blame, nothing more.

When later asked whether it had been difficult to persuade the prefect of his broad and fantastically greedy interpretation of the firman, Hunt showed no signs of remorse. "We succeeded," he said, "without great difficulty."

Thus, "without great difficulty," on July 31, 1801, a carpenter in the English navy, assisted by five crew members, scaled the columns of the Parthenon with his bare hands and, with the aid of ropes and winches, detached the most beautiful metope of the Parthenon.

A celebration with wine and gifts was held while the marble, detached from its original frieze, was still dangling from its harness between heaven and earth.

Like a pig strung up by its hooves.

Like a man hanging from a noose.

The next day, another metope was detached and transported to Piraeus.

And so on, stone after stone, until the titanic void of the museum where I find myself tonight was dug.

* * *

It's after one A.M., but I don't dare lie down on the cot I've left in a corner of the museum. I'm afraid to touch its hard aluminum frame. I fear that the cold metal will haunt my dreams.

One dream that recurred for decades after my mother's death: I'm having lunch with my father. She comes back to reproach us for all the messes and mistakes we've made in her absence. The deep sense of shame, the discomfort of having been caught in the act and exposed.

Uncanny, the perception that accompanies the thought of a deceased person, the conviction that they can monitor our actions from some heaven or the afterlife, can know our thoughts before we've even articulated them. The living condemned to be perpetually spied on by the dead until they're forgotten. Or maybe all of this is simply what you call remorse.

Crouched on the floor in front of what remains of the eastern side of the Parthenon frieze, I can't help thinking about what Phidias would say if he could see his marbles reduced to fragments: a foot in Athens, a head in Paris, a torso in London. Who knows what Pericles, who commissioned the works that would lead to the construction of the Parthenon, and everyone else, from Plato to Aristotle to Alexander the Great, would think if they saw this massacre.

And who knows what they would say if they saw me, barefoot and alone with the few crumbling remains of their world, leafing through the biography of its executioner.

The breach open, Elgin's emissaries caused an avalanche: one by one the most beautiful statues of antiquity were sawn off and detached from the Parthenon where Phidias had placed them.

Like jars of Greek olives, crates containing the works were stacked at the port of Piraeus, waiting for English ships to transport them to London.

Upon hearing the news of the removal of the first metope, Elgin was enthusiastic, to put it mildly: his mission appeared to be exceeding his wildest expectations.

Naturally, both he and the clergyman Hunt were perfectly aware of the suspect—read: completely illegal—nature of their work, closer to the work of a predator than a patron of the arts and education.

And although for a few months the world was too distracted to call them to account, the pair immediately began to fabricate alibis.

Not to lessen the humiliation of the Greeks, but to ease their own conscience.

The defense that Hunt, Lusieri, and the English workers in Athens went on to mount was that they had practically done Greece a favor: their decision to make off to London with the marbles was apparently motivated by the urgent need to rescue them from the devastation being wrought by the Turks, who continued to smash up the Parthenon undeterred. Dominated by the occupying Ottomans, Greece, they argued, lacked the might to protect its most personally meaningful and valuable treasures; so, the only solution was to take them away from Athens and store them in a safe place, even if they were thousands of kilometers away and under a foreign crown.

The premises of these arguments are clearly true—the future of the Parthenon, then transformed into a Turkish garrison, was highly precarious—yet the conclusions are unacceptable. It would be like saying that stealing from a defenseless child, or from a sick elderly person, is not only permissible, but one's duty. You don't shoot at the Red Cross. If anything, you help it get the most fragile and vulnerable among us back on their feet.

If you're really willing to accept the hypocrisy of their argument for coming to Greece's aid—aid, moreover, that was never requested—you still have to admit that two hundred years of kindly safekeeping what by birthright belongs to the Greeks is frankly too many. As the Greek minister Melina Mercouri, who fought tooth and nail for returning the Parthenon frieze to Athens, exclaimed, "The British say they saved the marbles of the Parthenon. Many thanks. Now give them back!"

Elgin's excuse in the face of accusations of theft was far less noble, far more childish. It was the French, he said, who started it.

Napoleon's ambassador Choiseul-Gouffier and his artist Fauvel *may* have tried on several occasions to send the ancient relics they found in Athens to Paris, but they never removed a single stone still firmly attached to the Parthenon. They may have wanted to, but they never dared.

That defense was certainly cheered by British public

opinion, which has always competed with France, but outside school playgrounds it doesn't stand scrutiny.

That said, in a way, it does contain a kernel of truth.

And something helplessly sad.

At the dawn of the nineteenth century, Greece was falling into a state of abandon and met with such indifference throughout Europe that it was foreseeable, crystal clear, that sooner or later someone would tuck the marbles of the Parthenon into his pocket and run off with them.

It matters little whether it was the French or the English or whether the marbles are now in the Louvre or the British Museum. The fatal attack on the integrity of the Acropolis and the eternal works of Phidias was merely waiting for a combination of favorable circumstances.

It could have been anyone.

It could even have been me.

Accidents and contingencies piled up around Ambassador Elgin.

Like a satellite dish, he intercepted all the greed of an unhappy, ravenous age, and would come to embody the curse of the Parthenon and all of Greece.

Elgin was still unaware that from each severed stone of the Acropolis Minerva's punishment would sprout like a poison fungus.

Moreover, at this point in the story, while the metopes fell one by one in his name, Lord Elgin had yet to set foot in Athens.

I feel like I can hear the heart of the night beating in Athens. Sleep has set down its semicolon and briefly suspended the lives of Athenians; when the sun comes up tomorrow, they'll go on writing.

Even the guard must have taken refuge from the disquiet of the night in a corner of the museum. Will he really stay alert till dawn, his eyes fixed on the Caryatids or the Moschophoros, I wonder, or will he end up dozing off, overcome by the extreme solitude of being in the Acropolis Museum after dark?

Maybe he feels heartened to know I'm somewhere on the third floor stretched out on my cot, the silent companion on his watch. Or maybe he's annoyed by the presence of a foreign intruder in his quiet, shadowy realm. That must be it.

For a second I think of all the night watchmen in their respective museums who, at this very moment, are watching over artworks at rest, exhausted after a day of sweaty hands coming dangerously close to them, vacuous comments, selfies no one will ever look at again. For the first time I think about how the night watchmen of museums, archaeological parks, collections, and foundations must also be added to the long list of so-called night owls, alongside the modern day lotus-eaters who populate night clubs, airplane pilots, garbage collectors, prostitutes, fishermen, new parents, security personnel at banks and ministries, doctors, thieves, murderers, and lovers.

I wonder if artworks, like men, breathe differently when

they're asleep. Which paintings sleep soundly as children? Which snore? Which suffer from insomnia? I imagine the wind-scented sleep of Botticelli's *Primavera* at the Uffizi; the nocturnal meditations of Leonardo's Vitruvian Man at the Accademia in Venice; the hieroglyphics into which the statue of Ramses II, at Turin's Egyptian Museum, rearranges the world; the erotic dreams of Venus de Milo at the Louvre. I chuckle at the thought of the trumpeting heads of Roman emperors, snoring in unison at the Vatican and threatening to rouse the Pope. The moans of Pompeii, the bewilderment of the Pergamon Altar as it wakes every morning and finds it's not in Asia but Berlin.

Do the marbles of the Parthenon, torn like hair from the skull of the Acropolis, still manage to get a little rest when the London rain beats on the windows of the British Museum? Or are they condemned to the violent insomnia of absence and emptiness?

Are their custodians in England, who at this very moment are on guard to prevent sadistic thieves from making off with Elgin's marbles, aware how ironic it is that they're keeping an eye on stolen goods?

The idea of sleeping hasn't even crossed my mind.

Besides, the cot I brought with me seems to be harder and more uncomfortable than Phidia's marbles; I might as well sleep on the floor.

But night in Athens is long, spending it alone almost a waste.

I think of the man who turned up below the museum windows at midnight to remind me I exist. He must be asleep by now. The image of his body above the sheets on this warm spring night makes me long to see him, almost lament the darkness that we're not experiencing together.

And then I feel jealous of his dreams, to which I'll never have access or be invited.

I don't know what to do to fill the time separating me from

the dawn that will rise above the Acropolis once again. It's not boredom but restlessness that plagues me. I don't know how to pay back this unique opportunity I've been granted.

So I decide to perform the same bedtime ritual that I have performed ever since I was old enough to do it by myself. Changing into pajamas in front of the Parthenon marbles proves impossible (though I'd thought about it when I prepared my few things for the night). But washing my face and brushing my teeth? That, yes.

The bathroom next to the entrance, with its sliding doors, motion sensors, and signs in Greek, brings me back to reality, with all its predictability and ugliness. Phew. The cool water is restorative, drawing my attention to the fact that my face is made of flesh, not marble; that Phidia's frieze will survive my inevitable disappearance from this earth.

I'm about to go back to my cot when, exiting the bathroom, along the corridor that leads to the Parthenon gallery, I find myself facing a large bulky stele with ancient Greek script. I can barely understand a word, having never studied epigraphy—another reason for my disappointment and frustration.

The museum label informs me that this is the balance sheet of officials who, in the year 440/439 BC, oversaw the construction of Phidia's masterpiece, the chryselephantine, or gold and ivory, statue of Athena Parthenos, which he envisaged as occupying the center of the Parthenon. Over one hundred and sixty kilos of gold were purchased that year thanks to the generosity of the Athenians, along with an equally large quantity of ivory.

I, on the other hand, stare at my bare toes and realize I haven't brought anything to offer Athena other than my fickleness. And my wet toothbrush now dripping on the floor.

* * *

In Civitavecchia, Italy, in the early months of 1995, a six-year-old girl saw the Madonna shed tears of blood.

A plaster statue, not much more than twelve inches tall and bought a few months before in the village of Medjugorje, had burst into tears in the little girl's backyard. The girl later claimed to have seen the Virgin appear and whisper terrible secret messages to her. After performing an exorcism to rid the statue of any demonic presence, the town priest shouted it was a miracle, and churchgoers from all over Italy gathered in the town to pray with the little girl at the feet of the Virgin.

Worried it might be a hoax and an abuse of popular trust, authorities ran tests on the statuette and found no devices or anomalies. And the blood flowing from the eyes of the Madonna, as copious as the ill omens threatening a sinful humanity, turned out to be of human (genetically male) origin. Although the Catholic Church has never openly commented on the alleged miracle, the niche where the statuette was placed became a shrine visited by hundreds of believers, and other Madonnas in Italy and elsewhere began to weep blood in unison.

In other words, the spirit of the Virgin, witness to too many horrors, had begun to bleed, and her bleeding never stopped.

Between 1801 and 1803, it was the very earth of Greece that was bleeding.

By day, Lusieri and Elgin's team hacked away at the Acropolis with saws and picks brought specially from Constantinople. By night, the scored and scraped marbles wept.

Reverend Hunt's intoxicated zeal drove him so far as to contemplate dismantling the entire Erechtheion with its portico of Caryatids and reassembling it piece by piece in England. Luckily there was no British ship in the Mediterranean available to transport such a heavy load, and the workmen restricted themselves to abducting just one of the six Caryatids, which they severed from its marble portico, like an artery from the heart.

Legend has it that on some nights the five remaining Caryatids can be heard sobbing over the vacuum left behind by their unlucky sister.

"Bringing the moon from her orbit" is how the archaeologist Edward Daniel Clarke described the shock of the Greeks as they watched with terror what the English were doing, certain that sooner or later the soul of the Hellenic land would have its revenge.

The most unsettling reprisal happened in Eleusis, a place where mysterious occult rites had been practiced for thousands of years and where there stood a colossal statue of Demeter still venerated by the villagers, who believed it was responsible for the fertility of their fields and abundance of their crops.

The citizens of Eleusis were alarmed by the arrival of over a hundred workers and fifty elephants sent by Elgin and set on carrying away the giant statue. They were convinced that the arms of the first foreigner who struck the goddess with a pick would be torn off. The night it was to be taken, with the ropes and pulleys already prepared at Demeter's feet, a strange incident was seen as a clear sign of divine punishment: a bull suddenly broke free from its yoke and gored the statue before escaping over the fields of Eleusis and making dreadful moaning noises all through the night.

The year after the Demeter statue was stolen, Eleusis suffered a poor harvest, and the following years still worse. For the peasants, it was confirmation that the enraged goddess had abandoned them. But Demeter exacted revenge on the British: the ship aboard which the statue was traveling sank in front of the white cliffs of England, and it took many years and a major effort to retrieve it. Today the statue lies forgotten in the corner of a museum in Cambridge where it barely manages to catch the eye, but in Eleusis its memory is still as alive as their belief in its curse.

Finally, where the gods failed, the French pitched in to obstruct the work of Elgin's emissaries. Almost every morning a French doctor stationed in Athens shut off the water to Lusieri's construction site, preventing the workers from cooling down and washing the marbles they extracted from the ageless Greek land.

Although the Parthenon marbles didn't ooze blood the way the Italian Madonnas did, limiting themselves to moaning through the night, there's no doubt that the damage done by Lusieri and Elgin's workers was violent and cruel and occasionally carried out with a savagery that bordered on torture.

What's dead is dead, it's true. But the grave remains.

Considering that at the dawn of the nineteenth century the ancient Greece of Homer and Plato had been gone for over two millennia, defiling its tomb was an offense nearer to sacrilege than to archeology.

It was just like the nighttime sacrilege done by people who desecrate gravestones.

The accounts of those who witnessed the butchering of the Parthenon metopes are particularly sadistic, describing blocks of marble brutally sawed off the frieze for which they were carved (the metopes aren't simply decorative add-ons, but integral parts of the building that Phidias designed), hitting the ground, and shattering into a thousand pieces thanks to the clumsiness of the workers and the difficulty of transporting them.

The drawings and watercolors that were made until Elgin's embassy arrived in Athens in 1801 depict a nearly complete Parthenon frieze. Those made after 1803 show a devastated landscape, one that appears to have been struck by a hurricane: the metopes and pediments have all but disappeared, blocks of marble resemble broken teeth, given the gaps where the stolen metopes once stood.

An Irish watercolorist, Edward Dodwell, who happened to witness Lusieri and company's destruction of the Acropolis, observed in his notebook: "During my first tour to Greece I had the inexpressible mortification of being present when the Parthenon was despoiled of its finest sculpture, and when some of its architectural members were thrown to the ground. [. . .] instead of the picturesque beauty and high preservation in which I first saw it, it is now comparatively reduced to a state of shattered desolation." Yet Dodwell himself left Athens carrying the head of one of the male figures of the west pediment, later nicked by an English sailor and lost forever.

As one ancient Greek myth has it, the Acropolis was a "place with no birds," in Greek ἄορνος (aornos), because no bird was allowed to build its nest on Athena's sacred rock.

The legend dates way back, to a time when the goddess was not yet associated with the famous all-seeing, all-knowing owl, but with the crow. It's a grim, murky tale. The three young daughters of Cecrops, the first mythical king of Athens, disobeyed a command not to open the basket carrying Erichthonius, the spooky serpent-child born when Hephaestus' seed was thrown to the ground by Athena. Horrified, the three girls leaped off the Acropolis and fell to their death. The crow raced to tell Athena the news, and the goddess, upset by the tragedy and furious that the animal had been so slow, forbade birds from ever flying over the Acropolis again.

Another version of the myth describes deep cracks on the Acropolis issuing poisonous gases that instantly killed any bird flying over them.

I don't recall ever seeing sparrows or seagulls flying around the Parthenon or nesting between the columns of the Erechtheion, and no owl has come to the museum window tonight to fix me with its round eyes.

The landscape suggests a piece of good prose: sober, polished, free of superfluities, pared down to its powerful essence. Whereas it is the infinitely wide sea behind the Parthenon that gives rise to an inexhaustible poem.

There is, I remember, only one other *aornos*, one other place where birds are forbidden in Greek mythology: Lake Averno, one of the gates of hell.

And that's where Elgin had just placed both his feet.

* * *

In April 1802, Lord Elgin landed in Athens for the first time.

What he saw was a despoiled, defaced Parthenon. By then most of the frieze's sculptures had been detached and loaded into giant wooden crates to be shipped to England. It was during Elgin's stay in Athens that perhaps the best-known sculpture in the collection was torn from the east pediment: the head of a horse pulling the chariot of the goddess of the moon.

It's ironic and sad to think that the person who initiated the theft of Phidia's frieze never saw it in its original location. Elgin was so taken with the idea of removing everything he could that he missed the most unforgettable and irreproducible sight— that of the Parthenon in its entirety.

Elgin decided not to stop at Attica's capital. Increasingly greedy and carried away, he ordered Lusieri and his followers to dig wherever possible, from Olympia to Mycenae, from Marathon to the monasteries around Athens, from Delphi to Eleusis.

His avidity was motivated by haste. It had been agreed that

his embassy in Constantinople would end in January 1803, and the peace between France and England had been signed, with Napoleon's eagle rearing its head over Europe and the Near East. So he had to proceed apace and remove everything that could be removed before the Turks, driven by the remonstrances of France, put an end to England's artwork binge.

As he sailed back to Constantinople in June 1802, the ambassador ordered his unskilled laborers to dig without wasting time and regardless of the cost. "I had slightly to become a barbarian," Lusieri wrote in a report on the theft of a metope that wound up destroying part of the Parthenon edifice. It was this mania, responsible for many foul-ups, that led to even more severe damage to the Parthenon. The stones quickly went from sniveling to sobbing.

But a new and serious problem was becoming apparent: stealing the marbles from Greece was one thing, shipping them to England another.

Payoffs and abuses of power may have been enough to get past Turkish authorities, but Elgin couldn't cast diamonds into the sea to guarantee smooth sailing and sturdy boats. In fact, the marbles of the Parthenon were so heavy and cumbersome that they couldn't be borne by most English ships passing through Greek seas, especially in a time of war and piracy.

The metopes sitting in crates in Piraeus faced a fate closer to that of junk goods from China stored floor to ceiling in a Shanghai warehouse than to that of Odysseus on his noble voyage. The marbles reached England via Malta, Alexandria, and Smyrna, independently of one another, taking different routes and leaving at different times, depending on the itinerary of the first ship willing to bring them aboard. And the number of shipwrecks in this story is staggering, almost too incredible to be true.

The collection was divided up. Some pieces too large to be shipped were cut into several parts. A few crates were lost for good, like boxes at the post office. Others were tossed into the sea due to bad weather.

Stolen sculptures accumulated more rapidly in Piraeus than those that set sail for England. Lady Elgin herself intervened to help her husband, using all her charm to convince the captains passing through Greece to take a vehemently unwanted load on board their frigates.

Because of these logistical issues Elgin decided to ship the stones himself and used his own brig, the *Mentor*, purchased as a passenger ship, to transport the Parthenon marbles to England.

Packed to the gunwales with crates and sculptures, the *Mentor* was commanded by Elgin's private secretary, William Richard Hamilton, who had already made a name for himself in Egypt by laying claim to the Rosetta Stone on behalf of the British. (The stone—*Rashid* in Arabic—is named after the place along the Nile where the French discovered it).

Around the time that Elgin was preparing to leave for Constantinople and Napoleon was entering Egypt, a French engineer stumbled upon a black basalt slab. The slab wasn't very interesting from an artistic point of view but valuable for its engraving of a decree from 196 BC in three different languages: Greek, Egyptian demotic, and Egyptian hieroglyphics. It was by comparing the three scripts a few years later, in 1822, that the French scholar Jean-François Champollion first managed to decipher hieroglyphics.

With the defeat of France in Egypt, the Rosetta Stone, which hadn't been transported to Paris yet because of the same logistical difficulties that Elgin encountered in Athens, passed to the British. It was Hamilton, in fact, who discovered the stele under a pile of rags in the house of a French general in Egypt and had it delivered to London, where it is now housed in the British Museum, right beside the marbles deported by his superior, Elgin. Over the years, Hamilton couldn't resist the temptation to embellish his role in appropriating the Rosetta Stone, going so far as to boast that he had rowed across the Nile until coming across a plague-infested French ship and risked his own life to rescue it.

On September 16, 1802, the *Mentor* weighed anchor from the port of Piraeus.

The ship carried seventeen crates of marble stolen from Athens, including fourteen fragments of the Parthenon frieze.

Two days later, the ship got caught in severe weather near Kythera, the island where Aphrodite was born, and sank to a depth of twenty-two meters. Hamilton barely made it to safety; this time he really had been in danger of dying.

It would take years to recover the shipwrecked marbles; involve dozens of workers, including sponge divers determined to snatch them from the seabed with their bare hands; and cost Elgin a fortune. The last fragment of marble was recovered in October 1804, over two years after the wreck.

Of course, a ship bearing the name Mentor was bound to have bad luck: in the *Odyssey* Mentor is one of the many guises of Athena.

But it wasn't Minerva's fury alone that cast a shadow over Elgin. The English ambassador would soon have to reckon with the unmistakable signs that he had incurred the wrath of the goddess of love.

* * *

All around me, night in Athens is pitch-black. The marbles and I ride out the same silence.

For the first time, I feel as if I understand the meaning of tragedy. Their stillness doesn't imply restfulness. What envelops the disfigured bodies of women, Centaurs, and horses is a sad, tired, wounded silence—the silence of someone at a loss for words.

These marbles aren't mute, they're cursed.

I worry that after a night spent at their feet, the curse will attach itself to me by osmosis and be passed on to my children—like the curse that afflicts Oedipus and all those who seek to know too much.

For the first time since entering this museum at the end of the day, the marbles of the Parthenon frighten me. Sleeping next to them seems sacrilegious.

At one point I think I hear a moan.

Maybe it's my insomnia, or a cat at the foot of the Acropolis.

Surely it's just the power of suggestion, yet I feel an immense weight of sadness sitting on top of me. And then I'm the one who wants to cry in place of the metopes.

I had wanted to write their story to make up for their disfigurement. How silly of me. As if sadness could be assuaged by writing.

I am curled up on the floor, next to the enormous window out of which the night hangs, like a black blanket wrapping the moon.

I observe the gigantic sculpture of Zeus' left hand holding a thunderbolt: the wrist is shorn from the god's arm and the fingers contract in empty space, like skeletal birdwings.

These stones know what the absolute tastes like, what it means to never give up.

In 1866 the *Atlantic Monthly* published a story entitled "The Case of George Dedlow." In it, the protagonist, a veteran of the American Civil War, wakes up in the hospital with a throbbing pain in his left leg. He tries to pull himself out of bed and call the doctor but realizes that during the night his lower limbs have been amputated.

The phrase "phantom limb" became a medical term around the same time, but stories of people missing limbs or parts of limbs and for inexplicable reasons perceiving their presence have existed since the Middle Ages. Generations of physiologists have grappled with the phenomenon, and it has been the focus of numerous twentieth century neurological studies aimed at figuring out whether our sensations primarily originate in the brain or in tactile organs. In other words, does the injured hand hurt in our hand or in our head?

Most striking are the unambiguous symptoms that patients who experience phantom limb report. Those who feel the missing limb do not experience fullness, consolation, or relief but rather a pain so excruciating that it often leads to madness. Some scholars call this "pain memory": the nerves near the stump remember the pain they suffered when the limb was amputated and relive it forever. It isn't bike rides or swims in the sea that the ghost of the missing leg remembers and longs for; it is the wound and scarring that keeps being felt again and again in a kind of parasitic memory.

In this sense, the drastic surgical solutions adopted to treat patients afflicted with phantom limb syndrome have had no effect: further cutting off the stump that it keeps remembering only causes the pain to return sharper and keener than ever.

Flesh and bone can be severed from the body, but the soul within it can't. Mindful, it never stops suffering from the separation.

For many months after the death of my father, I sometimes felt the urge to call him to talk about some trivial part of my day: the release of a book, an interview in some Italian newspaper that he would patiently cut out and put in a folder where he kept every article that mentioned his daughter.

Several times I went so far as to dial the number that I've known by heart for twenty years and that even now, alone in the middle of the night in the Acropolis Museum, I rattle off, like a whispered litany only the Parthenon marbles can hear.

Except then I remember that I'm about to call a dead father, a phantom father.

And then I have no other option but to hang up and remain inside my pain and silence before the specter of his absence drives me insane.

What hurts isn't the objective fact, the disappearance. It's the memory of it.

The memory of the excruciating hours after which all that

was left of my father was a plastic bag containing his few things that the nurses collected out of pity: a packet of tissues, his eyeglasses, the cell phone that I had tried to reach him on till the bitter end, the fruit he had promised to eat and, as usual, didn't.

Like a veteran missing a leg or an arm, in this new orphanhood I have a thousand more cheerful and positive memories than those last few hours, scenes that take me back to childhood. The Sunday afternoons when my father kicked around a ball with me in our backyard or taught me to swim, the time he ignored my mother's advice and bought me a dog. The day of my graduation in Milan, his awe at setting foot on a university campus for the first and last time in his life. The thesis that I dedicated to him and that he never read. The things he said to my classmates to hide his sense of inferiority—"I know Greek better than you, it's all thanks to me"—the glass of prosecco in the courtyard, the ridiculous jacket he insisted on wearing for the occasion.

The neurons that make up my brain have kept a record of this innocence, of the ignorance of that time when I didn't know death. But it serves no purpose.

The nerves connected to my heart remember nothing but the traumatic end, the amputation of my father from the life I live.

Since my father died, I am no longer a daughter.

I'm the stump of a daughter.

I find myself wondering whether the marbles here suffer this same cruel syndrome.

I find myself commiserating with them.

Maybe the severed hand of Zeus is experiencing the pain of his missing arm. Maybe the ankles of the maidens in procession feel nails being driven into their amputated shinbones and tendons, and all the vertebrae of headless Centaurs and warriors suffer from excruciating headaches that make them crazy.

So these are the ghosts that I've been summoned to share my night with.

The galleries of the Acropolis Museum aren't haunted by those annoying spirits of statues in the movies, who magically awaken in the moonlight. Instead it's the ghosts of limbs, hands, heads, horses' hooves and cow muzzles, stolen from Athens and taken to London, that inflict unspeakable torture on the stone limbs of the Parthenon.

* * *

Maybe to ease the pain and placate the ghosts that haunt the Parthenon marbles in front of me, it would be enough to rewind the tape, to reverse the amputation inflicted on the Parthenon. To return the heads, hands, arms, and backs to Athens and re-attach them to the frieze from which they were cut in the nineteenth century, in a grand act of restoration that would mark a turning point in the current debate over whether or not works of art should be returned.

That is exactly what the Greeks have been waiting for since the day of their independence, which was recognized by the London Protocol in 1830—ironic that the signature that paved the way for Greece's freedom was inscribed a few steps away from the marbles that Elgin confiscated when the country was still Turkey's prisoner.

"Give us back the *Gioconda*." So says the peanut gallery in Italy when it wants to express its mistrust of France, the country I have stubbornly chosen to make my home.

Unfortunately, ownership and flags are still the only yardstick for assessing who a statue or painting belongs to, and those objects would thus have rightful owners with passports, like any old car or pair of shoes.

However, exclusive property rights do not govern art, since

what constitutes a work of art is not only the object itself or its material—the canvas, the bronze—but also the ideas it inspires, which eventually form the artistic conscience of a people. What I mean is that the oil painting that we know as the Mona Lisa *is* the property of France, because it was Leonardo da Vinci himself who gave it to Francis I in exchange for an annuity. At the same time the artistry of the Mona Lisa is the undisputed property of the Italian Renaissance and the collective imagination of Italy, and that doesn't change, no matter whether the most famous painting in the world is housed in the Louvre, the Uffizi, or China, or has been pinched by Arsène Lupin.

We mustn't forget that the story behind a work of art doesn't end with the death of its author; on the contrary, it practically begins with its transmission. The Mona Lisa is an integral part of the history of the Louvre, and moving it elsewhere, as if it were a package bearing an Italian stamp—as certain crazy nationalistic positions claim—would be foolish.

But what do we do when the story of acquiring a work of art that dominates the halls of the most beautiful museums in the world, in London, Paris, and Berlin, was gotten by theft, looting, and imperialism? How do we address the shamefulness of Western museums where each work on display has a bloody skeleton in the closet, now that attitudes towards Napoleon's plundering—he had treated Italy like a giant flea market—and towards the unpunished plundering of the African continent have changed?

In this sense, it's important not to generalize and to make a clear distinction between works in European museums that were acquired legitimately (although perhaps they took place in times when political and diplomatic categories were far murkier than those today and the free will of one ended where the power of the other began) and those that plainly got there by theft.

Because we are not only talking about returning the work

of art itself, the patch of canvas stolen in the middle of the night or the piece of marble absconded with by the usurper: it is the collective imagination of a people that has been pillaged and humiliated. As in the case of Greece, which declares that it is unable to conceive of itself without the marbles of the Parthenon, an object that for the Hellenic people is the equivalent to what Shakespeare is for England or the Sistine Chapel for Rome.

In other cases, that same utopia that the Greeks perceive as having been violated and plundered was never even born, having been terminated by Western greed. Think of the many African countries where the absence of works of art, removed to the West during colonial occupation, has prevented them from constructing a national identity.

An estimated ninety to ninety-five percent of traditional African art resides outside of Africa, either in Europe or the United States. How can one even try to build a collective conscience after centuries of colonialism if almost every trace of what previous generations produced and passed on has been lost? How can students in Dakar or Bamako form an identity if the only museums they can access are empty boxes?

We're like dwarfs on the shoulders of giants, Bernard of Chartres once said. And yet there are whole populations for whom that giant was never even born, as is the case for certain African countries, condemned to artistic amnesia due to a lack of evidence.

Then there are giants that have been brutally browbeaten and thieved, as is the case of Greece, a country that is looking for the future from the damaged shoulders of its heroic past.

From a legal standpoint, works of art lawfully housed in European museums are untouchable: for no reason can they be transferred to third parties.

The rule of law therefore excludes any emotional appeals

for restitution. No government, not even the most Greek-loving, can do as they please with the catalog of the Louvre or the British Museum, returning artwork merely out of a sense of compassion.

In the United States, museums can sell whatever works they house in order to finance other projects (as the MoMA recently did when it auctioned off part of its collection—including Picassos and Rodins—to cover the cost of its digital initiatives), but in France no part of the country's artistic patrimony can be sold, not for any reason. It can't even be given away in the name of honor or out of respect for history.

In the past few years, given the persistent demands of African countries that artworks be restored to their barren museums, Europe has been forced to rethink the entire concept of what it means to own art and find solutions for speeding up the process of healing colonial wounds. In this sense, the 2018 *Restitution of African Cultural Heritage: Toward a New Relational Ethics*, a report authored by Senegalese writer Felwine Sarr and art historian Bénédicte Savoy at the behest of President Emmanuel Macron, marks an evolution in this debate and sets a precedent that could shape how European museums operate going forward.

After a series of trips across the African continent and meetings with people on the ground, the two scholars made recommendations to the French government that elevate the discussion around restitution and spare it from the meaningless remarks that come from irrational and emotional quarters. It isn't a matter of siphoning works from European museums to create museums of a national and nationalist bent—to Italy Italian art, to Senegal Senegalese art, to Athens Greek art—but rather of ceasing to play innocent or dumb about historical convulsions.

Instead of childish logistical maneuvers, the report suggests at least making visitors to our museums aware of the provenance of the painting or statue that they're looking at. It's about tracing the origins of art, something already mandatory for many foods and consumer goods. If we're all hyperaware of where the meat on our plate comes from, or the t-shirt on our back, shouldn't we also be worried about the circumstances by which a work of art has arrived in this or that museum in Europe?

The second recommendation of the Sarr-Savoy Report is based on the free circulation of works of art—i.e., they recommend loaning works of art when the law doesn't permit returning them.

Just as a Parisian can choose between alluring Asian art at the Guimet Museum, irresistible Pacific art at the Quai Branly, the devastating beauty of the Renaissance at the Louvre, and a thousand other works of art, so, too, should a citizen of Mali, Guinea, or Madagascar. *That* would make art truly human, truly global. The Nike of Samothrace, the Mona Lisa, the Venus de Milo, and other famous European artworks would suddenly be living like rockstars, touring in Africa, Asia, and the Pacific, greeted by hordes of fans in every city they play.

In 2021, in an unprecedented move, twenty-six works of art belonging to the royal treasury in Abomey, which were looted during the nineteenth century and kept in the Quai Branly Museum, were returned to the Republic of Benin. Legally speaking, France was forced to adopt a special bill in the National Assembly authorizing the restitution of the Beninese treasure. The bill only applied to those twenty-six works and does not, therefore, affect similar cases.

There are many other African works of art whose peoples are waiting for them to receive their ticket home.

Who knows if tonight, at the end of May, the marbles of the Parthenon sitting in the dark galleries of the British Museum, in the wing that once bore Lord Elgin's name, still have the wherewithal to wait and see Greece again. Or if they gave up hope a long time ago.

Waiting is terrible. Giving up hope is worse.

* * *

They can't handle them.
They don't have the resources.
Their museums aren't up to snuff.
Besides, nobody would go see them there, they're too remote. They're on the other end of the planet.
They'd end up losing them, you know.
Or having to resell them.

History, said Thucydides, repeats itself.
So do its hypocrisies, I'd add, still up at two in the morning in the Acropolis Museum.
For the first time I realize that the excuses for not returning the Parthenon marbles over the last two centuries are the same as those being made today in the debate over whether to return African works of art.
I'm beginning to suspect it's a curse of geography: every South is destined to be humiliated by some North, and there will always be someone higher up to remind you that you belong down there, at the bottom, head bowed, flat on your back.

"We did them a favor. The Greeks should thank us." For a long time that was the position of England and the West toward Greece's grievances, and it came with a healthy dose of paternalistic surprise at the country's lack of gratitude. Due to the Turkish occupation, so they said, the political situation had been too precarious, the marbles of the Acropolis would all have been destroyed, or worse, sold off again. "Lucky for humanity that they're safe in London."

Once Greece obtained its independence, people in Europe began alluding to the government's instability: "How can we trust them? It's a desperately poor country of shepherds and fishermen. They'd never know how to take care of a treasure that fragile and precious. They're unqualified to." And when the museum on the Acropolis was built in 1863 and the first archaeologists trained, people began objecting: "It's too small, it's not up to snuff, and Athens is too far away, on the edge of the world, the marbles are better off in London where more people can enjoy looking at them."

Over a hundred years later, in 2009, the new modern museum where I am spending the night opened its doors (free at first, just like the British Museum) and people remarked how "truly admirable" it was. "Maybe," they said, "we can lend you the marbles for a while." And when Athens rejected that proposal? "Well, clearly they don't want them."

Strange, this proposal of loaning Phidia's marbles to the country that produced them. It's like if someone stole my bicycle and when they got caught not only refused to give it back but claimed the right to lend it to me whenever it suited them.

As I write this, the board of the British Museum has yet to take a final stance on returning the Parthenon marbles, though that has been vociferously requested not only by the Greeks but by UNESCO.

English ownership of the marbles is deemed unequivocal and the work of Lord Elgin entirely legal on the basis of the firman he possessed.

Both sides rejected the idea of exhibiting 3-D replicas of the frieze so perfect as to seem real.

In a recent interview in the *Times*, the deputy director of the museum said he was open to the possibility of a long-term loan, the duration and method of which would be agreed upon with England. However, Greece balked at taking any step that might implicitly recognize England as the owner of the marbles.

Clearly I'm a weak person.

I don't have the patience of a chief in Benin. I have, instead, a certain propensity for shortcuts and lies. For imposture.

I might have accepted the loan.

But once they had arrived in Athens, once they'd been reunited with the broken stones I see in front of me, I'm not sure I'd have the strength to give them back.

I don't know if I'd have the strength to force the frieze to make a second one-way trip out of Greece.

To take or to leave, to keep or to give back. To tell the truth or live a lie.

Tonight this story of the Parthenon marbles seems less a question of art and more of an unhappy vocation.

That it has to do with imposter syndrome appears clear to me. Somehow my self-esteem has broken down, so that, in the eternal struggle between black and white and good and evil, I'm like one of these honest Lapiths arrayed in front of me, only I think of myself as a Centaur. Instead of attacking the enemy, I attack myself.

Admitting it doesn't help or comfort me. On the contrary, it leaves me indifferent in my daily struggle to hide my hooves and filthy mane from others.

"Imposture," from the late Latin *imponere*, "to make believe," is a horrible word. It refers to when someone maliciously takes advantage of other people's trust, and it doesn't admit excuses, unlike a lie blurted out in the heat of the moment or a white lie told with good intention. Imposture is the product of a tenacious, all-consuming, premeditated, surgical endeavor; it is the constant attempt to construct a story and stick to it no matter how false or absurd.

Unlike lies that stem from a momentary misstep, imposture requires a steadfastness so stubborn that, for those held hostage to it, it would be far easier, and much less tiring, to attempt to adhere to reality than to invent it.

In extreme cases, like when someone who has two different families in two different cities or who says they're going to work every morning and then wanders the streets all day, the effort it takes to constantly revise reality, as if reality were just a rough draft, is draining to the point of madness.

But it helps to know it's not fatal: You don't die of imposter syndrome. At the most you wind up in prison.

Sinister as it sounds, the term "syndrome" doesn't refer to a disease but a correlation of symptoms and circumstances that can be attributed to the same anomaly. So the good news is that imposter syndrome is not like schizophrenia or bipolar disorder; the bad news is that the risk of developing such a mental pathology is high.

As with almost all of the spiritual ailments of our times, the term is quite recent. It was coined in 1978 by two American psychologists, Pauline Rose Clance and Suzanne Imes, to refer to a psychological condition that leads to doubting oneself and one's capabilities. People suffering from imposter syndrome have difficulty accepting a compliment, attribute their successes to luck, are constantly afraid of failure, never feel legitimated in their work, and think that they don't deserve the positive things that happen to them or that they are ever really in the right place. This way of thinking, paralyzing as superglue, not only prevents people from enjoying their successes but holds them back from making progress, because they are constantly waiting to measure up to something—but it never happens.

So be it.

Tonight at the Acropolis Museum, like many nights before, I'm too tired to put my childhood on trial and go digging for a clumsy remark that my mother or father made that ruined my self-esteem, that made it grow warped and frail like a crooked twig instead of developing healthily so that whenever something good happened to me I could puff out my chest and think "I deserve it."

In the articles I've read on the subject, I've been struck to see that it's mainly women—over seventy percent of the female population—who suffer from imposter syndrome. Being a woman, I needed to interrogate my feminine side to find out what it is about my sex that makes me more susceptible to the parasite of insecurity.

In my case, I'm not so sure that I'd feel more comfortable had I been born a man. And in *any* case, I'll never know.

All I can do is divide the world into two categories: those who, faced with a problem, blame everything on the problem (I didn't pass the test because it was too difficult, so-and-so left me because they don't deserve me, etc.) and those who think they're the problem (I failed the test because I'm not smart enough, so-and-so left me because I don't deserve them).

I firmly belong to the latter batch of poor souls, aboard the same boat, taking stock of what can't be repaired.

What an awful thing, waste.

* * *

I don't know which category Lord Elgin belonged to but the fact that at one point he thought he deserved to own the Parthenon marbles leads me to believe he didn't lack for self-confidence. At least before the first manifestation of Athena's rage, as soon as he'd left Constantinople, in January 1803.

Determined to savor Europe after years in Turkey, before returning to London Elgin and his wife embarked on a journey that took them to Rome, Marseilles, and finally Paris. But after the rapidly shelved peace between England and France signed in Amiens in 1802, war broke out again the following

May when Napoleon ordered the arrest of every member of the British military on French soil. As soon as Elgin arrived in Paris, Bonaparte, who hadn't gotten over his grudge, had him detained on parole, on the grounds that he was a diplomat.

For the couple, what was supposed to be a few months' sojourn in France wound up lasting three years, until June 1806. Being held captive must have been traumatic and humiliating for Lord and Lady Elgin, but their life in France wasn't all that unpleasant. First installed at the Hôtel de Richelieu in Paris and then in the Southwest, they were only obligated to report to the police from time to time. The couple spent over a year between Pau and Barèges, a fashionable spa town at the foot of the Pyrenees, where the worldly and cosmopolitan life, filled with parties, games of whist, and concerts, was not so different from the one they led in Constantinople. During one reception Elgin had the pleasure of meeting the Count of Choiseul-Gouffier, the former French ambassador in Constantinople and the man who first raided the Parthenon. Elgin found the count charming and intelligent, if obsessed with recovering the collection of marbles he'd left behind in Athens (in an ironic twist of fate, that too would end up in London after the ship transporting it to Toulon was captured by the English).

It was at this time that the curse Athena cast on Elgin for desecrating her temple began to take its tragic shape.

In the autumn of 1803 and winter of 1804, the former ambassador was placed under arrest for a few weeks, first in Lourdes and then in Melun, under an inexplicable bureaucratic pretext which may in fact have been related to the Parthenon marbles, and separated from his wife, who preferred to go to Paris to try to intercede at Napoleon's court.

In 1805, William, the couple's fourth child born in France, died at the age of one following an illness, and Lady Elgin, already pregnant with their fifth child, lost her mind. In her despair, she was comforted by a young family friend, a wealthy English bachelor, who made a deal with Napoleon so that he could accompany her to London to bury her son. Nine months later, the two were lovers, and Mary Nisbet hastened to shed the title of Lady Elgin and ask for a divorce, as well as substantial alimony, setting off a scandal over which much ink was spilled in English newspapers.

Having lost his wife, Elgin was now left with his political ambitions—he was still a forty-year-old in the prime of his diplomatic career—and family fortune, but a dry-eyed Athena would destroy these two consolations with the same fury with which the ambassador had destroyed her marbles.

Upon returning to London in June 1806, Elgin received no recognition for the role he played in Constantinople. One by one, all the honors he coveted were denied him. He even lost the seat in the House of Lords that he had occupied for over fifteen years. Despite his entreaties, no political office was offered to him, and Elgin was branded with the prefix *ex-*—ex-husband, ex-ambassador—and relegated to the foggy Scottish countryside where he could meditate on the rubble to which his life had been reduced.

At least he still had the Parthenon marbles, Elgin must have thought. Even if he'd yet to lay eyes on that which had cost him so much. Back in London, they'd been piled up in fifty heavy wooden crates that nobody knew what to do with.

Sitting in this empty museum, I find the story incredible and outrageous: once they'd made it to London, the marbles sculpted by Phidias stood waiting, more like oversize moving boxes blocking a landing than glorious, rediscovered treasures.

During Elgin's three years in France, the marbles shipped from Greece were delivered to his mother. How many times has my father been forced to do the same, to collect the bits and pieces that survived one of my shipwrecked relationships?

But you don't just store fifty crates packed with Pentelic marble in a basement and wait for the recipient to pick them up. Not knowing where to put the marbles, Elgin's mother parked them in the garden of the Duke of Richmond, near Westminster, where they spent three English winters exposed to the elements as if they were garden gnomes and not Phidia's masterpiece.

Out a wife and a political career, Lord Elgin was impatient to at least recover the marbles for which he'd sacrificed everything and rent a large enough house to host them, but the economic damage wrought by his ambition was becoming catastrophic: the cost of retaining artists and laborers in Athens, acquiring the ultimately shipwrecked *Mentor*, and loading and unloading the marbles totaled nearly forty thousand pounds, or several million dollars in today's currency. Sure, in Constantinople Elgin had received gifts of precious stones and diamonds, but most of the fortune he accumulated in Turkey quickly evaporated given the many gifts he had had to give to local officials to see to his interests and with the colossal costs of his embassy delegation, expenses that at the time came out of diplomats' own pockets. In addition, the artists he'd hired in Athens demanded a lot and produced little. Particularly Lusieri. With his severe drinking problem and pathological love of women and gambling, he finished next to no sketches, while other artists sent London but a few views of the Acropolis.

In a matter of months, Elgin was destitute. He was forced to sell almost all the furniture in his home in Broomhall, lay off his staff, and withdraw to a few sparsely furnished rooms where he'd live alone. Unable to pay even the adjutants that had accompanied his embassy to Turkey, he was abandoned by everyone, even by the zealous clergyman Hunt, who, without a salary, never spoke to him again.

In the end, Elgin was stricken with an awful disease, a form of gangrene that left him tragically disfigured, like those ancient statues whose noses are gnawed clean off by time and savagery. Months later, in his indignant poem, Lord Byron would see Elgin's terrible condition as an unequivocal sign of Aphrodite's wrath: no woman would ever find the ambassador attractive again.

If intentions are measured by what somebody is willing to lose, we must acknowledge that, in the name of the Parthenon marbles, Elgin was prepared to lose everything.

In a wild reaction to his fate, the former ambassador decided to lose even more. In June 1807, he plunged further into debt by renting a large house with a garden on the corner of Piccadilly and Park Lane, determined to live alone with his marbles.

It took him nearly six months to open the crates and unpack the marbles, but now Elgin could look into the eyes of those Centaurs and Lapiths, those knights and maidservants sculpted by Phidias whose severed limbs I'm keeping watch over tonight in Athens.

Were it not an English story about the Parthenon marbles, it'd be a Greek tragedy. In under two thousand square feet Elgin amassed the ruins of Greece: sculptures, inscriptions, columns, and capitals were stacked one on top of the other, with no thought to marshaling them into a coherent whole. In the center stood the orphaned Caryatid, surrounded by pieces of the frieze arranged by size, from largest to smallest, and the heads of horses and busts of warriors were piled in a corner, like broken mannequins.

For a long time Elgin refused to come out of his hangar, the violated womb of the classical world.

Who knows if he was contemplating in silence the ruins of Athens or the ruins of his life.

Who knows if he thought, at least once, that it had been worth it.

* * *

It's *my* imposter syndrome, *my* deceit.

So I'll keep it.

I know it is owing to it that I live, write, and love with an intensity verging on obsession. That I live on the cutting edge of each day and year and never let a moment slip by.

Owing to it I'm free from the ignorance of my mother and father, emancipated from a sad and messy family tree that includes illiterates, peg legs, and a dearth of emotional intelligence.

Had I not thought that I deserved better, that I could be different, that I could risk more than the people who gave birth to me and whose blood I share, I would never have bothered to study Greek or Latin. Nor would I have written books and moved to Paris. I would have given up a long time ago.

Tonight it's me standing in front of these marbles, no one else.

If I'm masquerading as someone else, at least I'm doing it well.

So what if I'm not Greek, if I don't even know ancient Greek all that well. My masquerade worked and my refusal (however modest) to accept my family's ignorance seems like a triumph tonight.

I was determined to pursue difficult things, but at least they were big things.

I'm not the first and I certainly won't be the last.

All of Europe has done what I've done to escape an unworldly and pointless fate, and it continues to do it: for over two thousand years it has proclaimed itself the cultural heir and rightful guardian of Greek culture.

We take from Greece by the handful so that we don't have

to admit to ourselves that we descend from ignorant, forgetful people and that that is our destiny. To disappear like the dying breath of someone all on their own.

The cultural roots from which we say we descend, and from which we pretend the crooked world we inhabit descends, are not ours, but we desperately need to believe they are.

When Greece rightly points this out to us—it points it out to me, like yesterday evening at sunset, in the alarmed looks of the museum guards who couldn't believe I was granted such a privilege—we react with anger. And deep contempt. No, we object, they're the ones—the Greeks, Phidias, Pericles and the others—who are ill-equipped, who are children of a minor and fraught history, who are in need of help and protection.

Then we take a shot at being colonizers and custodians. We ransack Greece's ideas, marbles, and ideals and exhibit them in our grand museums and libraries. We lie to ourselves and others until we're convinced that they are ours. They belong to us, we claim. Why stoop to say thank you?

And when Greece dares to straighten her back, arrogantly embracing our own Western charade, we put her back in her place, on her knees, persuading her that she, the mother of the classical world, is no match for us. That she deserves nothing but our sympathy and spare change.

It's like the dwarf convincing the giant he's too small until the giant ends up believing it.

Like the barbarian calling the Greek stupid until two thousand years later the weary Greek agrees.

* * *

At the beginning of the nineteenth century one traveler,

passing the disfigured Parthenon, wrote in his notebook that he heard "a moan issue from the temple's offended spirit."

Two centuries on, these marbles still haven't stopped moaning. At this late hour, the gallery of friezes looks more like a war hospital than a museum. And my cot appears to me exactly what it is: a bed for invalids and casualties.

Maybe the merciful thing to do would be to put Athens out of its misery and tear down the little that is left of the Parthenon. To pull the plug on these one-armed soldiers, these hobbled horses, these fallen gods, and end their suffering.

I thought I could repair the marbles, as if they were shards of a broken vase. But maybe we ought to destroy them. Maybe that's the one way to get over our guilt.

We all enriched ourselves at the expense of Greece.

As long as these marbles continue to exist, they will remind us of our theft and hypocrisy.

They'll be our damnation.

Certainly, starting tonight, these stones will be the eternal witnesses of my own inadequacy. In a few hours the sun will rise on my insignificant reality.

How much pity I seem to feel inside me now.

And I'm not sure if it's pity for these mutilated marbles or for myself.

Any writer worth their salt knows that only a small fraction of literature can aspire to make up for the ugliness men have inflicted on the world.

I strongly doubt that by writing I will succeed, I who have seized on the pain of these marbles and this people because I couldn't take up my own.

It isn't a question of what nowadays we call cultural appropriation. I won't pretend to explain to the Greeks how to suffer. It's just that I want to be the one to suffer for everyone, at this hour, in the middle of the night, while Athens is asleep. It's the only thing that, insignificant as I am, I have to offer Greece. It's my sacrifice at the foot of the Parthenon. For these two hours or so that separate me from dawn, I hope and pray that all the sadness and all the emptiness contained in these broken stones will converge in me as if I were the lightning rod of human greed installed on the third floor of the Acropolis Museum.

If there is bitterness or regret in the Athenian air, may it strike me and not the rich dreams of the Greeks. Let them rest. Let them forget if they can.

And if there are curses stuck in the spaces within these stones, then for the next two hours I'll endure those too.

Ever since I was a girl, I've always marveled at the fact that the most important city in the classical world had chosen a female goddess as its patroness.

Over the years the figure of Athena, Minerva in Latin, has exercised a profound influence over me. I feel something like devotion to her. I was seduced by the fierce warlike goddess, her independence from family—born of Zeus' head, she never even depends on the womb of her mother Metis—the intelligence-cum-clairvoyance mirrored by her spirit animal, the owl. I even tattooed her impassive face on my left arm in a desperate attempt to give my youth more meaning. As I look back on it now, my infatuation seems obvious: I was like an orphan hoping to rebuild her life around an intelligence I wasn't certain I possessed.

In the mysterious Orphic Hymns, Athena is the goddess of wisdom for the good and the "inciter of madness and war" for the wicked.

Everyone knows who the villain in this story of stolen marbles is. What strikes me as incredible and extraordinarily cunning is the way Athena chose to take out her rage on poor Elgin: his punishment didn't arise from the dust left behind when the marbles were spirited to London.

No, the final blow came from England: the curse of Minerva bore the name and rhythm of Lord Byron's poetry.

Lord Elgin may "boast of having ruined Athens," Byron wrote in 1810 in his preparatory notes to *Childe Harold's Pilgrimage*. What happened in those few years under the Greek sun and English clouds seems like the stuff of dreams. Humiliated and plundered by England, Greece was compensated by the most famous English poet, so much so that it is in Byron's outraged poetry that we find the fuse that lit the revolt for Greek independence in 1821.

That's how it always goes, I think, facing a sculpture of the western frieze in which a young soldier tenderly strokes his horse's mane with its hooves raised off the ground as if it were flying. Suffering is therapeutic, what doesn't kill us makes us stronger, and every wound is a necessary prelude to deeper healing. Or so they say.

Life is written not with caresses but scars. It's the pages ripped out in anger that most impact our biographies.

We must kneel to misfortune with gratitude, making pain our teacher and guide. Because, as with the Parthenon, in life it doesn't matter so much what you lose. It matters what you do with that loss.

But first you have to realize that you've lost something.

In this sense, Byron's poem did to the afflicted spirit of the Greeks what the sun does to a field of red poppies after days of rain: it made their heads turn upward. And once they'd straightened up, after centuries of humiliation, they finally began to demand a reckoning for all that had been lost and stolen.

It seems like a paradox. Actually, it is. With Lord Elgin, England had taken away the Parthenon marbles, never to return them again. But in the bargain England lost its most romantic poet to Greece. By condemning the theft of those marbles, Lord Byron helped lead Greece to freedom, and died for the cause.

* * *

On his first trip to Athens, in 1811, Byron wrote his prophetic poem, "The Curse of Minerva." It was supposed to be published immediately after his return to London, but for reasons unknown (perhaps due to the intervention of Lord Elgin himself, who begged Byron for mercy several times to no avail), publication was postponed, though copies continued to circulate among intellectual circles—with neither the author's authorization nor his signature.

Last night at sunset I experienced what Byron describes in the beginning of "The Curse of Minerva." Night falls over Athens and the poet finds himself alone contemplating the mutilated remains of the Parthenon, reflecting on human greed and the melody of things.

Yet what appears to Byron isn't, as it was with me, the past and its shortcomings. Minerva herself comes to the poet. Yet her ghostly image is very different from that of the wise warrior goddess for whom the Greeks erected the Parthenon. Athena is a wreck: her peplos tattered, her face gaunt, her spear broken, her armor banged up. Instead of a war cry, out of the goddess' mouth comes outrage. "Seek'st thou the cause of loathing!—look around," she screams, and she shows Byron the mess that Lord Elgin has made of her temple, succeeding where neither the barbarians nor the Turks had.

The implacability of the goddess' curse on Elgin and all his descendants rises to the level of ancient tragedy:

> Without one spark of intellectual fire,
> Be all the sons as senseless as the sire:
> If one with wit the parent brood disgrace,
> Believe him of a brighter race:
> Still with his hireling artists let him prate,
> And Folly's praise repay for Wisdom's hate;
> Long of their Patron's gusto let them tell,
> Whose noblest, native gusto is—to sell:
> To sell, and make—may shame record the day!—
> The State—Receiver of his pilfered prey.

Athena's wrath doesn't spare England. She takes no pity on the country as she prophesies famine, political and economic crisis, popular revolt, and defeat on every battlefield. But she reserves the worst damnation for Elgin; like Herostratus, who dared to set fire to the temple of Artemis in Ephesus, he will be cursed forever, "loathed in life, nor pardoned in the dust."

I'm not particularly religious, but I am a spiritual person.

I believe in signs, in the irrational wisdom of presentiment and sensations. I have faith in life, if for nothing else than to will it to keep flowing.

Rereading Byron's verses now, at three in the morning in the Acropolis Museum, may be the most sacrilegious thing I've ever done. I'm the one alone with the marbles of the Parthenon, not Lord Byron, but Athena hasn't appeared to me tonight, like one of the many Madonnas in the country where I come from. There's been no sign, no aftershock that I can latch onto to make me feel, if not welcome, at least pardoned.

It's as though "The Curse of Minerva" is speaking to me and no one else tonight, me with my biography of Lord Elgin in my pocket, taking a form of pity on the ill-starred ambassador that I've rarely felt for a historical figure before.

Much as I'd like it, I now understand that in this story of stolen marbles, I will never fill Lord Byron's shoes, nor will what I write ever compensate Greece the way his poetry did.

Even if I did everything to free myself from my family, I am not the exceptional bastard child of that ignorant lineage that Minerva tells the story of. Tonight I realize, or maybe just accept, that I descend from people without intellectual depth, about whom Athena speaks with anger. And that will be the fate of my children and grandchildren and whatever else I'm able to produce and create.

Tonight, facing the Parthenon, I am just the last in a long line of Elgin's descendants who has thought of building her life on the ashes of the ancient world with the sole purpose of selling something—and sitting here on the floor, I don't think it matters whether what you're selling is a stone or a book.

* * *

Twists of fate or supplications to fate? In 1811 Lord Byron

returned from Athens to England via Malta aboard the *Hydra* and while the poet was writing his ferocious "Curse" on deck, the last marbles of the Parthenon robbed by Elgin's crew were traveling with him in the hold.

In March 1812, Byron's masterpiece, *Childe Harold's Pilgrimage*, was published in London. The first edition sold out in three days, becoming the first best-seller in modern literature and making its author a controversial and beloved celebrity on the scale of Andy Warhol or David Bowie.

There's only one harangue against an individual in *Childe Harold's Pilgrimage*, and that individual is clearly Lord Elgin. When the romantic protagonist arrives in Athens, the sight of the ruins of the Parthenon rouses in his heart profound anger at the perpetrator and sincere pity for the Greeks who were "too weak" to guard the sacred temple.

Within months, Byron's poetry was read and translated throughout Europe, gave back a voice to the marbles stolen by Elgin—which still lay stacked up in his warehouse in Piccadilly—and woke the public after a lengthy collective siesta.

The debate changed the discourse dramatically: it was no longer a matter of academic discussion surrounding the authenticity of the statues—their authorship had been frequently questioned then—or how to restore them, a job for which none other than Canova, the modern Phidias, had been contacted. (Fortunately Canova refused out of humility and respect.) The exposed nerve led public opinion to demand answers. People wanted to know by what right Elgin had snatched the most important works of classicism from a debilitated but proud people, removing them with saws and picks from a building that had stood intact for more than two thousand years.

No discussion of the Elgin Marbles can overlook Lord Byron's indignant verse. There quickly formed societies of wealthy Greek-lovers who demanded that the marbles be returned and Greece's honor repaired, and because Byron was then the most fashionable intellectual in Romantic Europe, excoriating Elgin became a favorite pastime.

A traveler returning from Greece couldn't avoid deriding the scandal done by the thieves of antiquities and the vulgarity of humbling a country that history had already humbled. Anyone who set foot in Athens had to criticize Elgin in their letters home, no matter that these same champions of the integrity of the ancient world would come back to Europe with fragments of vases or Greek sculptures in their suitcases. Some began to testify against Elgin from the comfort of their own living rooms without even bothering to travel to Athens. Among French travelers, their indignation was coupled with regret that the sculptures were not in the Louvre.

The names Elgin and Mary Elgin, which the couple had engraved on one of the columns of the Parthenon when the two were still in love, were seen as an example of their barbarity—and angrily scratched out. Perhaps people preferred to overlook the fact that the name Byron was carved into one of the columns of the temple of Poseidon at Cape Sounion, still visible today. Meanwhile, in opposition to the beauty of the Parthenon (*opus Phidiae*) the words *opus Elgin* were bitingly engraved on the rough brick column that the English ambassador's agents had substituted for the Caryatid sent to London.

So it was that, starting with the anger over Lord Elgin's having stolen the marbles from Greece, the philhellenist movement was born and became a fixture throughout Europe. Like a flower with various petals, the movement pointed in all directions: from championing the right to self-determination to taking up arms against the monarchy, from pining for the days of Napoleon to espousing the most liberal ideas. There were even sincere calls for repaying the debt owed to Greece that had accrued over two millennia.

"If I fall, I shall fall gloriously, fighting against a host," declared the almost mystical incarnation of philhellenism known as Byron. When the Greek War of Independence finally erupted in 1821 and European governments, surprisingly moved by what in principle was nothing more than poetry, took steps to send arms and soldiers, Byron went in person to Greece, having been commissioned by the Philhellene Committee in London to bring aid to the people who had risen up against the usurper.

The poet landed in Missolonghi on January 5, 1824, determined to raise an army of five hundred men, for which he would invest a good part of his own fortune. But after four chaotic months, on April 19, Easter Monday that year, Byron died of malaria at the age of thirty-six, not on the battlefield but in a sickbed.

Throughout Europe, the blood that Byron spilled on the noble earth of Missolonghi became the symbol of philhellenism and of the tears of a people who were finally liberated and avenged.

Thus, thanks to Byron's poetry, Greece was at least partially compensated for the humiliating loss of its marbles.

* * *

Shortly before Greek pride transformed into revolt, Athens and all of Attica had been reduced to an open-air bazaar: visitors and European government emissaries and royal families competed, with gifts and bribes, for archaeological finds that, like ancient magma, never stopped spewing from the eternal land of Greece.

Two flags rippled on the slopes of the Acropolis, one French and the other English. They flew over the houses of Fauvel and Lusieri, the artist/middlemen employed by Ambassadors Choiseul-Gouffier and Elgin, who had stayed on in Athens to oversee Europe's network of art trafficking.

However, in this mercantile climate that saw the Turks make incredible profits off what they regarded as nothing but old stones, stones with which Westerners filled public and private collections with priceless treasures, there began to take shape, for the first time in centuries, a fully Greek self-awareness and perspective. Somehow, out of the smoke that rose inconsolably from the ruins that European greed had left in Athens, Hellenic consciousness and a feeling of cultural belonging were reborn in this generous and injured people.

As if awakened from the collective amnesia enforced by Ottoman rule, the Greeks set about taking an active role in the archaeological campaigns carried out in *their* country in search of *their* art. Tired of standing by for ages and watching others dominate them, they started to regard Greek art and culture as products of their civilization that ought to be defended at all costs.

It wasn't just a question of defending their sculptures and their works of art from foreign invaders; even the ancient language and literature, knowledge of which had practically vanished during centuries of Turkish rule (apparently there was only one elderly guardian of ancient Greek in the years Elgin was in Athens), re-emerged from the broken marbles like a phoenix.

Obviously, the voracious West wasted no time criticizing this rebirth of Greek pride. The Greeks were repeatedly fed the paternalistic line that it was *for their own good* that their art was being shipped abroad; that they were being protected from their inability to look after them and from the sad political fate of a subjugated people.

Once again Byron was the first to align himself with the Greeks and demonstrate genuine solidarity. "Now, in the name of Nemesis! for what are they to be grateful? Where is the human being that ever conferred a benefit on Greek or Greeks?" he writes in the notes to *Childe Harold*, asking anxious

Europeans whether the Greeks really ought to thank the Turks for taking possession of their freedom and pay homage to the French and the English for stealing their art while intellectuals insulted them in their indignant articles.

The marbles and monuments now found in European museums, far from the resin-scented Greek wind, are but a fragment of the ones lost to the predatory frenzy of the West in those years. A vast number of sculptures and fragments have been swallowed up by the black hole of history, and we can't demand justice for them now; they're like victims whose killer hid their bodies.

A few years later, in 1821, the Greeks waged a desperate war to regain their dignity, driving out the Turks and taking back their place of honor among the nations of Europe.

From the very start of the independence that they fought body and soul for, Greece would devote itself to tending to its archaeological heritage with heroic ardor, like Antigone determined to bury her brother's body after it had been left to the dogs.

* * *

A Greek intellectual of the age was said to have predicted to a friend of Lord Byron: "You English are carrying off the works of the Greeks, our forefathers—preserve them well—we Greeks will come and redemand them."

And if tonight at the Acropolis Museum Greece were to reclaim what it has given me all these years, what would I be left with? Not much, I think.

My job, my home, my reputation, the friends I've made thanks to my books, my way of organizing the world, even my thoughts. If Greece took back what it has generously given me, I'd be left with nothing.

It would be the bankruptcy of my person. The ruin of the life that thanks to Greece I have fought tooth and nail to build.

Finally, exhausted, I gave in and lay down on my cot, harder and more uncomfortable than marble. I realize I forgot to bring a blanket and pillow, I have nothing to shield my body from the gaze of the night and the marbles of the Acropolis.

To fall asleep, rather than sheep I count my debts to the Greek people.

Material wealth isn't what I'm most afraid of losing were Greece to call in its debts.

It's that bitter heat that each of its stones gives off to comfort the fate of men.

That sense of humanity that we all struggle to define, unsuccessfully.

I've never understood how we decide that something is of value. From inside of us? Or outside?

The impostor I carry around inside me summons a weak, hazy image that so depends on the judgment of others that it needs to cheat, falsify, and lie.

The discourse around self-esteem has always bugged me, whether out of boredom or because it stings me to the quick I'm not sure. Yet I remain convinced that one's perception of oneself isn't drawn from some mysterious inner well but defined only in relation to the world around them and their fellow human beings. My perception of myself always needs a reward, a pat on the back: good girl, nice job.

Without that—I don't know if this sounds more pathetic or childish—I might die.

The fact that the perceived value of the Parthenon marbles has experienced similar fluctuations doesn't disturb me tonight, it consoles me.

If it happened to the monument that embodies the perfection of the classical world, that preserves that world's nectar as if it were an ancient bead caught in amber, why wouldn't it happen to someone like me who keeps thirsting for it like a suckling infant?

There was a time in the ancient past when these metopes and friezes, whose shadows I can barely make out in the night, were worth everything: during the perfect and unrepeatable fifth century BC when they were sculpted by Phidias and offered to the city by Pericles in honor of its patron goddess, Athena. As with all new things, their value quickly began to decline. People got used to the sight of them and then stopped seeing them at all. Meanwhile the vitality of the classical world around them—first Hellenistic, then simply ancient (read: old)—also declined.

For a thousand years the Parthenon marbles were in such decline that they were forgotten, left to languish on top of the Acropolis as a vestige of a lost age which people even stopped feeling nostalgic about. At the time of the Ottoman occupation, Phidia's sculptures were worth no more than ordinary stones strewn about the ground, but they began to gain in importance again at the end of the eighteenth century with the arrival of European tourists who were willing to pay to cart them off. If on the eve of the Greek War of Independence the cost of a pebble-sized piece of the Parthenon was quite high, then how much could Elgin's collection, still patiently waiting to know its fate in a dusty, damp storage space behind Piccadilly, be worth?

How can we put a price on fifteen metopes, seventeen pediment statues, and seventy-five meters of the Parthenon frieze sculpted by the school of Phidias and parked in a London garden?

Thinking about it makes my head spin.

A lot. A whole lot. Oodles of money. That's what I'd have answered has someone bothered to ask me.

But England decided it wasn't worth much at all.

So, after being despoiled, damaged, and finally shipped off, the Parthenon also had to endure being told it wasn't that valuable.

That, basically, it wasn't that great.

* * *

Strangled by debt, Elgin knew he had to sell his collection of ancient stones to the English government: he could no longer afford to exhibit them to the public for free, and the recognition for his work that he'd so hoped for from the English government had never materialized. As early as 1810, the former ambassador had entered negotiations to have the works appraised, but they fell through when Parliament offered him thirty thousand pounds, less than half the costs Elgin had incurred to transport Phidia's works to London.

In 1814, immediately after Napoleon's abdication, Elgin again nurtured the hope of selling the marbles to the English government so as to recoup at least some of his fortune and dignity. One would have expected—I would have expected—that the people of England and the royal family would all fall on their knees at the first glimpse of the glorious sculptures of the Parthenon and start kissing the hooves of the Centaurs as if they were the feet of saints. But no, public reaction to the masterpieces was tepid: in the wake of the indignation aroused by Byron, those who did not despise Elgin and what he did hesitated to recognize that the marbles were priceless. Beautiful, sure, but not sublime. In the academic world there were many people who, more out of envy than ignorance, questioned the authenticity of the sculptures, or in any case didn't consider them worthy of the ancient works found in Rome, like the Apollo Belvedere or the Belvedere Torso.

Heartsick, his pride in tatters, Elgin was prepared to do anything to see the beauty of the Parthenon marbles finally acknowledged in England, but the articles and pamphlets he published had an even more adverse effect.

London might not take him at his word, but it would believe Europe's greatest art connoisseurs, Elgin must have thought when he asked Ennio Quirino Visconti and Antonio Canova for their expert opinion. Visconti had directed Rome's Capitoline Museums before becoming the conservator of antiquities at the Louvre, accompanying the Italian artworks that Napoleon had carted off to Paris; Canova needed no introduction. For Elgin, and the Parthenon most of all, these men's opinions were both an aesthetic and moral salve: they recognized the splendor of the frieze and the metopes, whose value surpassed any Roman copy, and were certain they were the work of Phidias.

Finally the wind seemed to be at Elgin's back, perhaps for the first time in this tale of old stones and bad luck. With Bonaparte now in exile, all of Europe was talking about works of art to be returned and museums to be filled. The Congress of Vienna of 1815 was firm in its decision to make France return the more than five hundred works stolen by Napoleon to their respective countries, primarily Italy (though almost half remain missing to this day). The only power that found itself wanting for famous works in its museums was England, which suddenly became interested in the Elgin Marbles again—and didn't dream of returning them to Greece, as was the fate of the works stolen by the French emperor. And while English artists were discovering the beauty and value of the Parthenon marbles at last on public display at the house in Piccadilly, the Prince of Bavaria sent Elgin a blank check for the purchase of the entire collection, which rattled England's Parliament and compelled it to hurry up and make an adequate financial offer.

Everything seemed to be going swimmingly for Lord Elgin, who was cheerfully compiling the first complete catalog of his collection. However, out of the Pandora's box of wooden crates that had been used to ship the marbles to London came Minerva's curse, and it spread like a gas, wreaking havoc and causing pain.

The beginning of the end was marked by a parliamentary commission whose aim was not to establish the value of the Parthenon marbles, but to determine by what right if any Elgin had taken possession of it at the expense of Greece.

***

The Select Committee began its work on February 29, 1816.

Elgin was interrogated for two days. During his testimony, the former ambassador summed up the most widely talked about story in England in frank and simple terms: before leaving for Constantinople he had been advised to contribute to the development of English art by going on a mission to Greece; when the Crown refused to finance the project, he continued to pursue it at his own expense; given the precarious state of the Parthenon while under Turkish occupation, he had requested and obtained a permit authorizing him to take the marbles and bring them to safety in London. End of story.

The committee pressed him on the legality of the firman granted by the Ottoman authorities, especially considering that Elgin couldn't produce a single original document, not in English or Turkish or Greek. They'd all been lost, he told the committee. There was only one anonymous copy in Italian. Various witnesses, including Elgin's then secretary, supported his claims that he had acted lawfully, but more than the paperwork, what swayed the court were the astronomical costs that the former ambassador had voluntarily taken on for nearly twenty years.

"I have been actuated by no motives of private emolument," Elgin asserted, and the committee had no trouble believing him when it saw the total cost of the Parthenon marbles and the debt Elgin had racked up in every bank in the Mediterranean, sometimes at exorbitant rates: 74,240 pounds, equivalent to several million pounds today.

Elgin mounted an honorable and dignified defense before the committee, as a man who had been slandered in public and lost everything and more in Athens. But this was deemed insufficient. Next, the most illustrious English artists were called in to establish the value of Phidia's marbles, which they almost unanimously agreed were the most superb works ever to be seen in England and would inspire the arts for centuries to come. Then travelers who had had the privilege of seeing the Parthenon before and after Elgin's work were summoned as eyewitnesses. Many of them preferred to concentrate on Turkish rather than English barbarism, since they too had left the Acropolis with souvenirs of various sizes in their pockets. An emotionless Hunt—he who had hand-delivered the wretched firman to the Greeks—confirmed Elgin's words, from first to last.

Naturally, not a single Greek was called to testify or express an opinion. Pretty strange for the trial of an alleged murderer to overlook the victims. Determined to evaluate whether it could buy the marbles from the person who stole them from the Parthenon, England never had the (at least intellectual) scruple to conceive of ever returning Phidia's works to Greece. The committee was, in fact, more interested in learning about what actions the French took in Athens, and relishing in their envy, than in concerning themselves with how the Greeks felt or the legality of their own country's actions.

A verdict was reached a few weeks later. It was a short but detailed document that found the actions of Her Majesty's former ambassador as being well within the bounds of law. And therefore there was nothing to prevent the sale of the marbles—even if the English government was prepared to pay no more than thirty-five thousand pounds.

The sale came as a crushing blow and bitter disappointment, yet Elgin had no choice but to bow his head and accept the humiliating deal. Parliament voted in favor of a law that would transfer ownership of the Parthenon marbles—and responsibility for their detachment from the Acropolis summit—to Britain.

In August, as the summer sun in London was already veering toward the gold of fall, Phidia's sculptures were relocated to a temporary room at the British Museum—a room named, appropriately, for Lord Elgin.

* * *

"A most dizzy pain" is what a twenty-one-year-old John Keats felt upon seeing the marbles of the Parthenon exhibited in the British Museum.

Lord Elgin must have experienced the same agonizing dizziness in his final years, which he lived in the wide abyss between success and damnation. Aesthetically speaking, his mission in Greece was by any measure a triumph: the neoclassical style, with its Doric and Corinthian colonnades, architectural designs taken directly from the Parthenon and the Erechtheion, as well as Hellenistic sculptures of all shapes and sizes, cropped up on every street corner in London. Personally speaking, however, Elgin's biography was reaching its final pages, and they didn't promise a happy ending.

Divested of the marbles that had begotten his misfortune, the former ambassador had nothing left but pain and outrage. But even that wasn't enough to arouse Minerva's sympathy.

Of the thirty-five thousand pounds agreed upon for the sale, over half was withheld to repay part of the debts he'd incurred. The rest barely covered more urgent expenses. The letters, each more anguished than the last, that Elgin sent to Parliament to attain a paid office, or at least a pension, remained unanswered. On the contrary, the British government ordered him to refund a portion of the income he made as an ambassador, which it retroactively deemed too high.

Meanwhile in Athens Lusieri, now an old rheumatic man, continued to live on the slopes of the Acropolis off the money that Elgin had paid him every month for over twenty years. Occasionally the painter sent him some gem or other, including one haul of over six hundred ancient vases. Despite his financial hardship, the ex-ambassador never abandoned his lifelong friend to his fate, and was still waiting to see his drawings, the one reason the artist had been hired over two decades earlier.

In 1821 Lusieri was found dead in his room overlooking the Parthenon, but all that surrounded him were empty wine bottles; apparently, in those twenty-plus years of activity, Lusieri had only finished two drawings. After a tireless search complicated by yet another wreck at sea, Elgin recovered only one of Lusieri's watercolors, one that depicted, ironically, the least interesting ancient monument in Athens.

In 1821 Lord Elgin also bumped into his longtime nemesis, Lord Byron. Once again it was a matter involving Greece that brought the two men together, though this time they found themselves on the same side, since both Elgin and Byron were among the first champions of English philhellenism.

Finally, the one who had exiled Athena's marbles was himself forced into exile: Elgin spent the last years of his life in France, where he had taken refuge to escape his creditors. In November 1841 he died alone, disgraced, in Paris.

And, as in any Greek tragedy worthy of the name, his mistakes redounded on his offspring, who were forced to pay the debts that their father had accrued over thirty years to get his hands on the Parthenon marbles.

* * *

So, that is the end of the story. The story of the Parthenon marbles missing from the Acropolis Museum.

But stories aren't made of marble, they're made of sand. No tale, not even this one, is definitive or immutable. It goes on living and being rewritten every time it's told.

Today the Parthenon is a universal symbol of what is missing, of a void. Of all that has been abandoned to neglect and plunder. Of all that we didn't know how to defend, or that we forgot to, so that it was divvied up, sold off, shipped away.

But the story hasn't come to an end the way my night at the Acropolis Museum is coming to an end. There are still many pages to be written—about remedies, reparations, solutions. Maybe even restitution.

The present is the blank page in the future history of Greece. The hand and spirit that will write it are ours.

If tonight I needed words to fill the void left in Athens by Lord Elgin, it was mostly to relieve my own incompleteness. To exorcise that curse that has tarnished us all since the very first stone—material or intellectual—was pinched from Greece.

I don't know if they've forgiven me, but at least the Phidian marbles have listened to me tonight.

I feel I've done my part, however imperfect. As each of us tries to do.

When I wake up, what will await me is the eternal spectacle of Greece that rises out of the darkness night after night. True to its task of revealing the emotion that the world contains and helping people believe they contain a little of it themselves.

The salt of the Aegean restores me to life, stinging my skin and eyes.

It's only ten o'clock, but the beach in Vouliagmeni, less than twenty kilometers from Athens, is already beset with cheerful Greek families resolved to make the most of the hot sun and inviting sea on the last Sunday in May. On the horizon the silhouette of Aegina looks like a mirage, the sky is fatally blue, the white sand is the same that 2,500 years ago the Greek heroes sank their feet into.

I dive into the sea again and hold my breath. The silence underwater reminds me of the night that I just spent at the Acropolis Museum. From this morning on, I'll miss it, I'll search for it in every nook and cranny, determined as a fisherman hunting sea urchin.

A mother's womb—that's how Homer described the sea lapping at the keels of ships in aquatic silence. To put the marble womb of the Acropolis Museum behind me, I've found no other solution than to immerse myself in the Greek sea. The eternal return to life at sea, Odysseus might have said; a pagan baptism of sunscreen, colorful lounge chairs, and restaurants serving grilled fish.

My eyes red from salt and lack of sleep. My mascara from the night before running down my cheeks, like the rusty tears of old statues. My body stiff after three hours of lying on a cot. More than the weary return of the survivor, more than the epic ascent from the underworld, leaving behind the Acropolis Museum was as violent as being banished.

Following the museum director's instructions, at dawn a guardian came to wake me up and clear the room that houses the Parthenon marbles before the tourists arrived. He wasn't the guard from the night before: there was something austere about him, and the superior way he scowled at my cot and my few belongings scattered on the ground made me think of snooty pedestrians in Paris dodging the bodies of the homeless lying on subway grates.

In any case, I'd already been up for a while, ever since the first rays of the sun came spilling through the windows of the museum as unmistakable as the miracle of life.

I used to think the sunset was the most unforgettable spectacle that the Acropolis had to offer worshippers over its twenty-five centuries. I was wrong. The real phenomenon is the dawn, which every morning illuminates the Parthenon, the daytime moon of this Eastern city.

For Homer, dawn is *rododaktylos*, rosy-fingered, but this morning it caressed the Athens sky with gold. Rising from Macedonia and Thessaly to the east, around six o'clock the chariot of the Sun showered Attica in golden light and like the descent of the Holy Spirit breathed new life into all its inhabitants.

I knew that Athena has always protected Athens and will always protect Athens. I didn't know that she was also her city's formidable director of photography.

Passing through the museum door, the happy early morning air in Greece reminded me of when I was a girl and used to exit my house very early to arrive on time for Greek Lit at the cloisters of the University of Milan. I'd like to show the untried student that I once was this radiant morning when, like a lover, I slip outside the Acropolis Museum at sunup. And tell her that all the pain and suffering was worth it.

Then I think of my father, of how in his dotage he seemed like an infant, and smile at the sky and feel firmly inside me the legacy of every one of his defeats.

There aren't many pedestrians crossing Dionysiou Areopagitou at this hour, mostly amateur photographers drawn to the light rising like a flag above the Acropolis. With difficulty, lugging the heavy cot that I did my best to reassemble, I climb the stairs and exit through the museum courtyard.

The yellow mailbox is still there. I'm surprised by my surprise at its presence, as if I were seeing it after a long journey. While the guard is counting down the minutes till my final expulsion, I slip my postcard in the slot, entrusting it to the industriousness of the Greek post office.

Then I turn around and see him.

The man who waited patiently for me at midnight at the foot of the Acropolis is standing on the other side of the street, straight as an ancient soldier. He comes toward me, picks up the cot, and hugs me without saying a word, without spoiling everything.

We call a taxi and go to the beach.

* * *

I don't know what I'll remember about this night tomorrow.

As I gathered my things, I gave a parting glance at the rubble of the Parthenon. One day I'll come back to the museum, of that I'm sure, just as I've been there before, but never again will the statues of Phidias belong to me as they did during these hours of the night.

I will spend the next months and years concentrating, my hands trembling with the memory as it escapes me, on making a mental copy of the contours that I glimpsed tonight. Complete, inviolate, restored by the story that I wanted to tell.

Their story. And the story of Lord Elgin.

Facing the fullness of Greece, we're all like the chipped stones of the Acropolis. We're nostalgia itself.

The age when the Parthenon proudly stood atop Athens in one piece is distant and gone forever, but the Acropolis remains the stage set where our thoughts take shape.

Human beings err, and court discord and misfortune, when they scramble to find a common element within themselves rather than look at what's behind them, at the pages of history. At Greece.

As in the receding landscapes of Renaissance paintings by Leonardo and Raphael, with their tiny bridges, hills, and trails in the middle and background, ancient Greece continues to be the scenic backdrop in which our faint ideas turn into movement and volition.

There, in Greece, our tears, our wars, our triumphs, and our griefs play out.

Where we truly *are* is in the shadow of the Parthenon, while in the foreground of our forgetful present we come and go.

What comes to mind is a question that occurred to Giorgos Seferis while he was gazing at the Acropolis: where are they now, the souls of all those people, of everyone who built these monuments?

Their souls, I suspect, have become our souls.

Acknowledgments

The book I brought with me to the slopes of the Parthenon was *Lord Elgin and the Marbles* by William St. Clair, one of the most powerful stories I've ever come across.

Quoted material from Nikos Kazantzakis' *Zorba the Greek* is from the translation by Peter Bien (Simon & Schuster, 2014); that from Emmanuel Carrère's *The Adversary: A True Story of Monstrous Deception* from the translation by Linda Coverdale (Vintage, 2017). Melina Mercouri was quoted in the article "Melina and the Marbles," which appeared in *The Sunday Times* on May 22, 1983.

I would like to express my sincere gratitude to the Acropolis Museum, its director Nikolaos Stampolidis, curator Anna Vlachaki, and the entire staff for making me feel welcome on the night of May 28, 2022. I will always cherish the honor bestowed on me and spend the rest of my life in grateful disbelief.

Thanks to Katerina Xyla-Loth, president of the Center Culturel Hellénique in Paris, and to the entire Greek Embassy in France for having supported me and made this literary adventure a reality.

Thanks to Alina Gurdiel, Manuel Carcassone, and Raphaëlle Liebaert for believing in this book and for their constant support while I wrote it.

Thanks to Nikos Aliagas for his friendship à la grecque since my arrival in France and for the photos he took at sunset at the Acropolis Museum, which serve to remind me that it wasn't all a dream. Thanks, too, to Sylvain Tesson whose show on Lord Byron at the Théâtre de Poche in Paris rekindled my philhellene spirit.

And thanks to my partner for waiting for me in front of the Acropolis that night, and for all the other nights—those past and those still to come.

Europa Editions UK

Read the World

Literary fiction, popular fiction, narrative non-fiction,
travel, memoir, world noir

Building bridges between cultures with the finest writing from around the world.

Ahmet Altan, Peter Cameron, Andrea Camilleri, Catherine Chidgey,
Sandrine Collette, Christelle Dabos, Négar Djavadi, Deborah Eisenberg,
Elena Ferrante, Lillian Fishman, Anna Gavalda, Saleem Haddad,
James Hannaham, Jean-Claude Izzo, Maki Kashimada, Nicola Lagioia,
Alexandra Lapierre, Grant Morrison, Ondjaki, Valérie Perrin,
Donatella Di Pietrantonio, Christopher Prendergast, Eric-Emmanuel Schmitt,
Domenico Starnone, Esther Yi, Charles Yu

Acts of Service, *Didn't Nobody Give a Shit What Happened to Carlotta*,
Ferocity, *Fifteen Wild Decembers*, *Fresh Water for Flowers*, *Lambda*,
Love in the Days of Rebellion, *My Brilliant Friend*, *Remote Sympathy*,
Sleeping Among Sheep Under a Starry Sky, *Total Chaos*, *Transparent City*,
What Happens at Night, *A Winter's Promise*

Europa Editions was founded by Sandro and Sandra Ferri, the owners
of the Rome-based publishing house Edizioni E/O.

Europa Editions UK is an independent trade publisher
based in London.

www.europaeditions.co.uk

Follow us at . . .
Twitter: @EuropaEdUK
Instagram: @EuropaEditionsUK
TikTok: @EuropaEditionsUK